ASPECTS OF THE CHURCH

ASPECTS
OF THE CHURCH

By YVES DE MONTCHEUIL, S.J.

Translated by
Albert J. La Mothe, Jr.

FIDES PUBLISHERS ASSOCIATION
CHICAGO, ILLINOIS

Nihil Obstat: Rev. Robert Pelton, C.S.C., S.T.D.
University of Notre Dame

Imprimatur: Leo A. Pursley, D.D.
Apostolic Administrator
Fort Wayne, Indiana

Published originally in 1951 by Les Editions
Du Cerf, Paris, France, under the title, *Aspects
de L'Eglise*, in the *Unam Sanctam* series. Nihil
Obstat: G. de Broglie, S.J., Sept. 10, 1947.
Imprimatur: Petrus Brot, Vic. Gen., July, 1948.

Manufactured by American Book-Stratford Press,
75 Varick St., New York, New York

55

Contents

1

The Problem of the Church

I. *It is of vital importance to know the Church*

I want to help you understand the place that the Church should have in your lives. As things stand now, you already live *in the Church*. However, you should come to the stage where you are always more and more *of the Church*. To do this you have to know the Church, to know her in her most profound reality. We should know not only what any attentive observer outside the Church can find out about her, but we should obtain the kind of knowledge of her available to the man who looks at her with the eyes of Faith.

We are able to rise to God only because He has come down to seek us out. The inevitable consequence of this is that we can be united to Him only by the means which He has determined for us. We may not choose according to our own inclination and make ourselves a pathway to Him according to our own tastes. We have to follow

frightening importance

servile fear
filial fear

1

the path He has marked out for everybody. There is no other way; outside of it we can only go astray. This path is the Church—not any church, but the Church as God instituted her with the characteristics which mark her off.

Since this is so, we have to take account of the Church in our spiritual lives. If anyone disregards the Church through his own fault, he is off the path of salvation. On the other hand, anyone who adheres to the Church but does not reap the fruit which is the product of this adherence—anyone who claims to lead his Christian life in his own way, without being at all concerned with the Church, or trying to learn what she is so that he might conform himself to her—such a man, too, is laboring under a delusion. Lack of knowledge excuses those who, through no fault of their own, cannot rise out of that ignorance. But we are enlightened enough already on this matter of the existence and necessity of the Church to which we belong so as not to have any excuse on this score. It is our duty to strive to know her intimately, in her essential elements, with a view to building the edifice of our Christian lives on the true foundation she provides.

By the Divine Will the Church plays a definite role in the return of man to God. We have to know what this role is, and that simply means that we have to know the doctrine of the Church. Now it would be wrong to get the impression that this doctrine will consist of involved issues, hair-splitting, or long drawn-out inquiries into subtle points. Not in the least! Like all religious teaching, it is a light on the road of salvation for those who have to walk on that road.

You see, then, that it is of vital importance for each one of us to know clearly just what the Church is.

II. Starting-point: Belonging to the Church is the specific characteristic of Catholic religious life

We will start off our inquiry by putting down a definite statement of fact. When someone looks at a Catholic to find out what there is which is distinctive about his religious life, or else when a Catholic considers his own case in order to compare his form of religion with other forms, one of the things which stands out most forcibly is this characteristic of "belonging to the Church." This is not because in other religions this idea of a church is completely lacking. In fact, there is probably no religion which, in a more or less broad sense, has not given rise to a church. This is doubtless a phenomenon based on the very nature of religion. But yet it is this very notion of belonging to the Church which is the most distinguishing mark in the case we are considering. Catholicism is distinguished from all other forms of religion, Christian or non-Christian, by the importance which it gives to the Church. In Catholic religious life, the Church holds more of a place, and that not only materially speaking; more than that, the very nature of the relationship of the Catholic with his Church is of unique importance. This is so because *where the Catholic is concerned, the Church governs his religious life not only from the outside, but also interiorly*. She is not like a shell intended to protect him. She is not an organization designed to provide a channel for some energy coming from the outside, precisely in order to control the flow of this energy. The Church is at the very source of this energy. In her we draw on this energy and through her we are united to the very source of this energy.

It has been fashionable to oppose inspiration and technology. The latter, by "pouring off," as it were, this inspiration, by forcing it to take on a definite form, and to give life to some material activity, enables it to produce tangible and lasting works instead of vanishing without leaving any traces. Along the same line, Bergson distinguished in religion a static element and a dynamic element. Indeed, there is no dearth of notions of religion in which whatever the individual has to contribute—whether he has drawn it from himself or whether he has received it from God—is readily likened to inspiration, the dynamic element. Since the activity of the spiritual society is therefore compared to the operations of technology, the static and stabilizing element, men can recognize its great usefulness, even its necessity, but they do not see in it the source of life and of motion. This is precisely the attitude that a Catholic cannot accept. The Church is for him *not only the principle which rules life, but the principle which passes on life*.

Although it is characteristic of all of Christianity to say that we can enter into contact with God only through Christ, yet the Catholic adds that we can come into contact with Christ only through the Church. (We are only stating here a principle and are considering the normal state of affairs. Later on we shall examine how and in what measure it is possible to enter into contact with Christ without passing, in a visible way, through the Church. Every Christian, whoever he may be, has to explain how, in certain cases, it is possible also to communicate with God without going visibly through Christ—unless he wishes to condemn irrevocably all those who, for some reason or other, have not known Christ. But of course, no Christian today wants to do this!)

III. *It is through the Church that we attain to Christ*

It is, indeed, through the Church that we reach Christ.

1. *Dogma is in the Holy Scriptures.* St. Augustine wrote: "I myself would not believe in the Gospel, if the authority of the Church did not lead me to do so." (*Contra epist. Manich. c. 5*). This formula does not express merely a personal opinion. It has to be adopted by every Catholic. Without a doubt, reason alone can succeed in recognizing that the Gospels were written by men in good faith, who had had the opportunity of knowing the facts which they narrate—and we can regard that fact as sufficient to compel an examination of the solution which Christianity offers for the religious problem. And if this examination were to be pushed to the limit, it would result in the proper atmosphere for proving how well-founded this solution really is. At any rate, it is only after we have accepted the Church along with the guarantee of divine inspiration which she teaches us to see in the Gospels, that we can be fully assured that the Gospels give us a true picture of Christ, and enable us to unearth something of the mystery of His Being.

The evangelists are certainly well-informed and sincere witnesses, as we said before. But, out of the whole sum of the actions and discourses of Christ, they have chosen to give what seemed to them to throw light on His figure, to make His message and role better understood. If, perhaps, they themselves had misunderstood Him, then the actions and words which are recorded might indeed be told exactly, but yet might carry a false significance because of omissions or errors of perspective. In place of the real Christ there would be substituted a Christ deformed by misunderstanding disciples. But if we reject the guarantee which the Church gives, what are the odds that disciples like the ones depicted for us in the Gospels, themselves penetrated the mystery of Christ? The more we see Christ as a unique Being in the history of humanity, the less can we expect to have a satisfying portrait of Him. And it is precisely the most precious aspect of His Being which would be in danger of being lost. For it is that very aspect of a personality by which it transcends its surroundings which most often escapes its contemporaries, or which they interpret most erroneously. If then the Church did not give us a guarantee that the evangelists were guided and sustained by a divine inspiration so that they would not be so far unequal to their task as to become untrustworthy witnesses in spite of themselves, we would be forced to base our knowledge of Christ on the echo which He awakened in the souls of the witnesses of His life. No matter how admirable that echo might be, it could not be sufficient for us. It is Christ Himself that we want to reach. In this matter it is the Church, and the Church alone which enables us to have complete confidence in the evangelists themselves.

Expressing the same idea in another way, we could say that, according to Catholic teaching, when Christ ascended into heaven, He did not leave behind Him one or more books containing His doctrine and His precepts. He did leave a Church charged with the task of prolonging Him. The Gospels did not exist before the Church. No matter how we go about explaining their origin, it is certain that they appeared in the bosom of the Church. They are the expression of her faith in Christ. They are the inspired interpretation (which is therefore infallible, not only as a whole but even as to details), of the life of Christ, of this work which God came on earth to accomplish. The Gospel is a teaching of the Church concerning Christ, a teaching of special and unique value. If we join to it the other writings of the New Testament, which are in their own way commentaries on the Event which introduced divine life into the world, we can say that all that the Church has to teach us about Christ is therein contained.

Of course this would have to be made explicit, and very precise, in order to defend it against the errors which would arise in the course of the centuries. But the Church would neither change nor add anything. Nevertheless, it always remains true that this knowledge of Christ comes from the Church and that, as a consequence, the Church is always present in those actions by which we unite ourselves to Christ. When we meditate on the Gospel, for example, not only do we get from the Church the texts, the words, the narratives which are the subject of our meditation, but as a matter of fact our very meditation on them is guided by the light she gives us. She it is who discovers the true meaning for us. Our personal effort is to be applied not in finding out the meaning, but in making it part of our lives. In fact, Revelation, the word of God, passes to us through the Church. Faith consists in believing God on His word, and God has spoken to us through Jesus Christ, Who is His substantial Word. It is through her that we can come to the true meaning of these teachings, of that teaching which He is Himself.

The Church fulfills this role in different ways. Sometimes she solemnly condemns an error which threatens to spread among the faithful. Sometimes, after a more or less extended period of time, she defines a controverted question. Sometimes, the truth of some point of her doctrine breaks into the light, spontaneously to a certain extent, either from the continuity of the teaching of her authorized representatives, or from the unanimous acceptance of her children. Be that as it may, it is impossible to possess the truth legitimately if we refuse to receive it from the Church. Once we have understood in what manner faith is the basis of our relationship with God, we realize the position the Church has in our lives, since we cannot even preserve our faith in God if we refuse to listen to the Church, and since the man who possesses most fully the spirit of the Church penetrates most deeply into the meaning of the Word of God.

2. *In the moral order*. But that is not all. Faith is only the beginning of a transformation of life. It can of course exist without that transformation, dwelling in the soul like a mere stepping stone. But it has no other reason for existing than to result in this transformation. Its purpose is not merely to enrich the understanding with a new knowledge. It prepares us to receive a new life, and once that has been received, faith sheds light on it to allow it to achieve a new intensity. Living faith is expressed in what we traditionally call "good works." But once again, it is the Church that tells us what works faith ought to produce. The Church is the teacher of morality as well as of dogma. This very word "morality" stands a good chance of being inadequate here, considering the limited meaning which is usually attached

to it. In current language it means hardly more than the "elementary works," if we may use that phrase, those works whose opposites constitute a sin for all Christians, those works which are the very minimum below which one is forbidden to fall.

Nevertheless, it is not only in the major phases of our spiritual life that the guidance of the Church is necessary for us. The Church is also the teacher of perfection, and the higher up we go, the more necessary it is to have her for a guide, because the road becomes more difficult to make out and the danger of illusions becomes greater. The greatest generosity can get off the track. The errors of spirituality which the Church has had to condemn were not all due to laxity, but they were not for all that any the less harmful for souls tending to perfection. And so, a system of spiritual doctrine emerges from the tradition of the Church which, while leaving room for even very diverse schools, in its essential elements is clearly defined.

3. *In the Sacraments.* This new life is not only a new direction given to our activity, nor does it consist only in living in conformity to the moral law. It is a participation in the very life of God. Through it we become sons of God, really and not metaphorically—although without any title to it on our part and purely gratuitously—by sharing in the life of the only-begotten Son. But once again, it is through the Church that we receive this life which sets up such an intimate relationship between God and us, and it is only through the Church that we are able to receive it. In order to be initiated into this life we must receive the Baptism which the Church gives and which brings us into the Church.

"No one can have God for a Father, if he does not have the Church for a Mother," says St. Cyprian.

What happens if someone should lose this divine life? In order to regain it, it is necessary to beg God's pardon through the Church, and this pardon could not be obtained while trying to do without her. She is present and plays an active part in the return of the prodigal son to his father. The same is true for the other Sacraments. The Eucharist, the nourishment for this life, is entrusted to the Church which distributes it to us. The union of a Christian man and woman is holy only if the Church consecrates it. The Church dispenses the Sacraments. Of course, she neither creates them nor modifies them, but preserves them intact in the manner willed by the Christ Who instituted them. Just as she is not the source of the truths of faith—for she has received them from Christ and her task is only to preserve them from all alteration, from injuries which might come to them with the passage of time, from the misunderstanding or the bad faith of men—in like manner she is only the guardian of the sanctifying will of Christ and of the rites which He has established to make this will efficacious. Yet it remains true that without the Church we would not know what the essential rite of the Sacraments is, nor what the true means of grace are. Outside of her bosom this sanctifying Will would not reach us.

There is in the administration of every Sacrament a "minister" who is indissolubly both the minister of Christ and the minister of the Church, and who cannot be the minister of Christ if he refuses to be the minister of the Church. Also, in order that the rite conferred be valid, let alone licit, in order for it to be more than a mere gesture, the minister of a Sacrament has to associate him-

self with the Church, either clearly or obscurely, explicitly or implicitly, even though it be only by his intention
of "doing what the Church does." Although there have
been discussions about the manner in which this intention ought to be expressed and about the qualities which
it should have to be adequate, nobody has questioned
its necessity. Every one admits that its meaning and its
basis is simply to connect the minister with the Church,
the unique dispenser of the Sacraments. A Christian
who knows the position which the Sacraments hold in
the Christian economy sees at the same time how deep-
seated is the function of the Church in his own spiritual
life.

IV. *The presence of the Church in the life of the
    Christian*

This presence is lasting and not transitory. It is an
active presence, an intervention in everything that produces, develops and expresses the Christian life. It is
not merely a pedagogical necessity destined to pass away
in time. The Church is not a mother whose children
need her only for a time, and who can then dispense
with her to deal on their own with Christ and with God
once they have reached maturity. She is not a mother
from whom one is separated in the measure that he
grows up. We can say, on the contrary, that the more
one is united to Christ and the more deeply he enters
into God, the closer he remains to the Church, the more
he acts under her direction, the more he yields to her
spirit. . . . No one, no matter how advanced he is, can
pride himself on receiving doctrine and life from God
without going through the Church. Therefore, she has
not been instituted only for those whose weakness

would prevent them from going on alone. She is not meant to accompany and guide us only at the beginning of our journey. This indwelling of the Church in the spiritual life (the depth and intimacy of which indwelling we have just tried to grasp), is something lasting and definitive.

The Church is visible, and not purely spiritual. A bit further on, we are going to point out the divine character of this Church which is present in our spiritual life in the way we have just indicated. But we will have to beware of reducing her to something invisible, to a spiritual society of souls united to God, and this out of an ill-advised desire to spiritualize things. On the contrary, she has a visible element, and this is so not only because she is made up of men whose very nature requires a visible element. She is visible precisely as the Church.

She is visible, first of all, by her exterior delineation, if we may speak in that way. Belonging to the Church, in the ordinary course of things, is not a purely internal accomplishment. It is based on the reception of Baptism, which is an external rite requiring matter and words, and conferred by a visible minister. Entrance into the Church is not brought about merely by a divine decision which in itself is not visible to the eyes, but sensible only in its consequences—by the transformation which it introduces into life. Of course it does result from a decision of God. No one enters into the Church on his own initiative. He is received into her, and he is not chosen by men for this reception, but is called by God. Yet this call of God, this being received by God, is expressed in an action which is like the visible body of this call, and is an action of the Church, namely, the administration of Baptism. A man remains in the Church as long as he agrees to profess her faith, which means *doctrine* adhering to a definite statement of belief expressed in formulas chosen and consecrated by the Church.

If, then, it is a fact that the faith by which the baptized person remains in the Church is not something purely external (nor even something purely human, since it is above all a gift of God), it is not on that account a wholly interior disposition lacking all exterior manifestations. Of course, even without actual Baptism and without exterior profession, it is possible to belong to the Church. But it is nevertheless always to the visible Church that one belongs, even though in such a case it is in an invisible manner, thanks to "Baptism of desire" and "implicit faith."

The Church is also visible in her hierarchy. Those who *hierarchy* make it up can be recognized as belonging to it because of a visible rite. They have been appointed in an external way. The ecclesiastical hierarchy is not a hierarchy of spiritual values which God alone would know, or which men could only guess at, each according to his own individual existence. Once it has been constituted, the hierarchy exercises its teaching and sanctifying mission, again through visible means such as the Sacraments and formulas of faith, and not only through prayers and interior acts which would remain hidden in souls.

And so it is that the Christian is attached to a visible Church. It is to her that he assigns the position we have tried to outline clearly. And the Church is uncompromising with regard to this position. She declares that she is the only one qualified to occupy such a position in a man's life. She is not one of those organizations a man can take or leave. She does not say: "Since the individual cannot lead his spiritual life alone, he must be associated with a church. Let him make a choice, then, among those which claim to be so many ways to come to God." Definitely not! She claims to be the only way.

She is nevertheless a means of immediate communication with God. In order to avoid a misunderstanding of everything we have said, we must insist on this other characteristic. With all her demands, the Church affirms nonetheless that she is not, and must not be in any way, an obstacle to the interior and personal communication of a soul with Christ and with God. We can, and we even must say, that she is a necessary go-between; we will call her a mediatrix in the sense that without her and outside of her, God cannot be reached. But we would have to avoid using those terms if we ran the risk of giving the impression thereby that the soul communicates with God only mediately, without any direct contact. The Church affirms on the contrary that it is precisely this very direct contact which is created through her. We should not compare her to a messenger who sets up communications between two persons who cannot meet, by going from one to the other. She is rather a facile medium which assures direct union between two beings.

In a sense, this is the whole problem—and we could say the paradox—of the Church, that she is at once constantly present during the dialogue between God and the soul, that she actively intervenes in this action, and that in spite of this she in no way detracts from the intimacy of this dialogue, that she in no way obstructs the immediate communication of the soul with God. If we make the Church out to be nothing but a grouping of souls which, each on its own account, communicate with

God, or if, on the other hand, we give up trying to make each individual soul enter into contact with God, we get rid of the paradox, it is true; but at the same time, we depart from Christian truth.

V. *The Church, a supernatural reality*

Thus we have what could be called the Problem of the Church in the life of each Christian. But, at bottom, that is a problem only because we are looking for a human solution for something which, on the human plane, does not admit of any solution. If the Church were only a human reality, she could never maintain at one and the same time this double role which Christian teaching assigns to her. But the Church is a supernatural reality. And so, it is necessary to speak of a *mystery*, rather than of a problem, of the Church. If then we want to be able to give the Church the place which she demands in our life, we must begin by convincing ourselves of her supernatural character.

We insisted first on her visible character, and this was necessary in order to forestall some system of eliminating her from the whole spiritual life while pretending to keep her there, a system which would consist in seeing her as a purely spiritual society. But without retracting anything that we have said, we must now bring to light a complementary aspect. It often happens that we consider the Church from a point of view which is too human. It is true that we see in her a society whose aims are transcendent, not temporal, a society instituted by Christ, and not by men. But in our eyes she seems to differ from other societies more by her origin and by her aims than by her very nature. But let us recall what we proclaim in the *Creed: "1 believe . . . in the Holy*

Catholic Church." The very existence of the Church can be known only by faith. We say, as a matter of fact, not only that we believe in the institution of the Church by Christ, in the necessity of belonging to her to be saved, in her all-embracing worth, but that we believe in her very existence, in her reality.

But, someone may object, anyone can prove the existence of the Catholic Church. It is a fact which all non-believers admit. To make our point clear, let us compare the Church to Christ. The comparison is all the more natural since there is a perfect harmony between the two of them. The unbelieving Jews saw Christ, they heard Him. That is to say, they ascertained the existence of what was visible about Him. Yet we cannot say that they believed in Christ, that they knew Christ, that they truly understood what He was Whom they saw, since they saw in Him only a man among other men. Only the faithful disciples—even if they did not as yet have at their disposal adequate formulas for their faith—who saw that Christ was the Word made flesh, that He was the Incarnate Son of God, knew Him truly. Only they had the right to say that they knew Who He was.

In like manner, unbelievers can ascertain the existence of this society which is called the Catholic Church. But, seeing in her only a human society, they do not know her, for they do not consider her as a supernatural reality which, while having a body, is not limited to this body. For us who have the faith it is necessary to form the habit of always considering the Church as a spiritual reality, a supernatural reality which is made manifest by means of a body. This body, this visible element, is part of her. It is indispensable for her existence and for her activity, just as the body of Christ was essential and indispensable for Him. But she is not only that. She is much more. The thing that gives meaning to the humanity of Christ is its union with the Word, so much so that we cannot say that he who knows Christ only as a man knows Him even partially—we should rather say that he does not know Him at all. In the same way, the man who sees only what we can call the sociological or juridic reality of the Church, the exterior organization by which she more or less resembles other human societies, that man does not half know her; he does not know her at all.

To know the Church, just as to know Christ, the light of faith is needed. We have to believe in the mysterious reality whose visible organization is only a necessary manifestation and serves as a mere envelope. And so we are right in saying that the Church has been instituted by Christ, recalling thereby that she has from Christ the traits which characterize her in her sojourn on our earth. But the Fathers were also right in saying, for example, that the Church was born from the side of Christ dying on the Cross, recalling in this way that she has with Christ more than the relationship of a society with its founder, as is the case with human societies. *If the Church is a sanctifying force, it is because she is a spiritual reality which could arise only from the redemptive death of Christ.* (It is important to understand correctly the meaning of this expression "birth of the Church," in order not to set it in opposition to another affirmation, namely that there was already a certain presence of the Church in the world under the Old Testament. Here we are not envisaging a relationship of time. We are indicating a source, that to which the true being of the Church, her existence as a supernatural reality, must be attributed).

2

Kingdom of God and the New Israel

I. *Some expressions used to designate the Church*

Both in the inspired writings, and in the works of Tradition which comment upon them, we find some very diversified expressions used to designate the Church. She is the "ark" which saves us from death, just as Noah's ark, at the time of the Flood, was the only means of salvation. But yet, we do not have the same relationship to the Church that passengers have to the ship which carries them; for we make up the Church, we are of the Church. Again, the Church is a "people," a congregation. But yet, Christians do not make up the Church by the fact of their coming together—she is certainly not formed by their union; one becomes a Christian only by being received into the Church. She is also a "mother" who brings us forth to a new life. But she is a mother who keeps her children within her womb. Her union with Christ is so intimate, so thoroughly does she draw her life from Him, that she is His "body." (Both the term "body" and the term "people" indicate the mutual union of Christians; the term "body" emphasizes the mutual interdependence, the need for one another, and the unity which exists amidst a diversity of functions; the term "people" indicates rather the personal character of the relationships and the harmony which is not imposed but free and willed).

Because in her Christ is present, because in her and through her alone man can offer to God a prayer which will reach Him, a worship which will be acceptable to Him, a worth-while sacrifice, the Church is a "Temple" —she is the temple of God built of living stones. Then, not only because she receives her life from Christ, but because there exists between Him and herself a mutual love which unites persons, she is the "Spouse" of Christ. Because she is at the center of the divine Plan, and consequently of world history, because she is the culmination of a preparation which has been going on since the Creation and whose essential element was the choosing of a people to carry a message, she is the new "Israel," the spiritual Israel of which the first was only the figure. Because in her are contained—veiled but really present— those riches the unveiled possession of which will be our joy for all eternity, she is the Kingdom of God, the *Kingdom of God* upon earth.

We must not see in this great number of terms— though I do not claim to have uncovered them all—an incoherent outburst of confused ideas. We must not see in it only the result of research, or of assorted individual insights. Since they are found in the sacred authors or else are consecrated by Tradition, it is because they were formed under the influence of the same Spirit, and they concur to make up a well-knit whole. Without a doubt, the link binding them is not of a logical nature—it would be vain to think of reducing one to another, or of organizing them into a system. From this logical point of view, we must say that they cannot be reduced one to another. But they all have to contribute to give us an idea—not indeed an exhaustive idea, but one which will be at least sufficient with a view to behavior—of what the Church is. There is not one of them which does not, in its own way, clarify the attitude we must have towards the Church, and the place we must make for her in our lives. We are allowed to choose some favorite point of view, but no one of them can be neglected with impunity. In fact, one of the essential characteristics of religious thought is that the object it has in view is infinitely rich to the point that it overflows our intellect and requires that we give it many expressions if we do not want some important aspect of it to remain in the dark.

imperfect

These terms are doubly deficient. First of all, each one of them expresses only insufficiently the facet or the relationship that it seeks to present. We have to look at it from a distance to get its full import. For example, the Church is more necessary for salvation than the Ark was for the bodily safety of the contemporaries of the Flood. Her unity surpasses that of a body or of a people. Christians are more indispensable to one another than are the members of the same body or the citizens of the same nation—and yet the spiritual life of each one, if its ultimate depths were sounded, would be more original, more individual, more personal, than the intellectual, moral, etc., life within a human group. The relationship between Christ and the Church surpasses in intimacy and in mutual devotedness whatever the most intimately united spouses have ever been able to realize.

The second deficiency comes from the fact that each of these terms only expresses one aspect of the reality, and must be complemented by the other aspects for fear of error; and as a result, not everything that is implied in a notion otherwise judiciously used, can be applied to the Church. Therefore, whoever would try to build up a theory about the Church taking as a starting-point any particular one of these terms which designate her—People, Temple, Body—would on the one hand be applying to her concepts which do not fit her, and on the other hand, would be neglecting essential aspects of the reality she is. In fact, in order to know how to understand these different terms, which elements to keep, and in what sense to expand them, all this demands that we have recourse to the living commentary which the Church herself makes on them. We must take her for our guide.

The reader can see that if we herein commit ourselves to preferring one or the other of these terms, it will not be at all to the exclusion of the others. In commenting upon it, we will not let ourselves forget the others; more or less implicitly and with more or less completeness, we will make reference to them. It is obviously impossible to make them all the object of extensive comment. This must be borne in mind, first of all so that no mistake will be made concerning the scope of what we are going to do; but also—and perhaps above all—so that you, the reader, may be enabled to get an idea of the Church which will be worthy of her. The Church is not something within our range of knowledge, or something we could contain in our minds, and understand in the manner that we understand some human object; we will never make a complete inventory of her riches. She will always be a *mystery* to us. We can only know enough about her to guide our Christian life and base it on truth, thus preparing ourselves one day to contemplate the Church in all her splendor.

II. *New Israel and Kingdom of God*

We will limit ourselves in this conference to the two terms *Israel* and *Kingdom of God*, one of which directs our thought towards the preparation which went before the Church and which transforms by filling it with new substance, the other which directs our thought towards the goal she in part anticipates in her very sojourn on earth.

Through the Church, the world returns to the Creator

Let us recall first of all that the Church forms part of the order established for the return of creation to God. Then, let us find her place in the divine plan as a whole.

God did not abandon fallen creation, but wants to bring it back to Himself. But it is through the Church that this return has to be brought about. That means in the first place—and above all—that she brings men back to God by tearing them away from sin and sanctifying them. But, though it is true that in Creation everything is for *men*, nevertheless there are also *things*, and, through the mediation of men, all these things also have to be brought back to their original destiny. The Church has blessings for most of them. She blesses not only "objects of piety," but also what we call profane things:

harvests and flocks, houses, cars, factories . . . whatever in nature serves man, whatever nature produces, can be presented for the Church's blessing.

It is true that too many Christians twist the meaning of this blessing or do not see its fullness. Sometimes they seek in it only a means of getting certain material advantages. But their lack of understanding does not destroy the deep meaning that the Church attaches to it. It is the consecration of the world. It is the affirmation that this world (which in the original plan of God is given man to enable him to know Him and to rise up to Him, but which has become for the sinner an opaque veil as well as a means of satisfying his guilty desires), has to be restored to its primal mission—consecrated anew by man to the service and glory of God.

"The Church," says Fr. Charles (*Missiologie*, pp. 85-88) "is the divine form of the world, the only rallying-point through which all the work of the Creator returns to the Redeemer, the only junction at which the Redeemer Himself enters into possession of His eternal heritage. . . . She is the sacrament of the world, the formulation of the adoration of the whole universe, the meeting-place of creation restored to the Word Whose work it is, the divine meaning given to earth. . . . The Church's mission is to invade the whole earth visibly, by her peaceful infiltration, in order to make it holy and return it to its place in the eternal liturgy of oblation." St. Thomas says of the Church that she is the "*reditus creaturae rationalis in Deum*" (cf. Congar, *Esquisses du Mystère de l'Eglise*, p. 69), and we can easily admit that this phrase says everything, since by God's Will, the rational creature is introduced by means of its body, into a world from which it is inseparable.

But for us who, being so often victims of a misunderstood spirituality, so often separate the soul in order to
oppose it to the world (when it is a question only of
tearing it away from the evil which corrupts it), it is
useful to underline explicitly this broadness of view as
to the Church's role. The Church brings about the sanctification and redemption of souls by making them
share in the life of Christ, both in the present order of
things and also for the life to come. But she also has
the role of sanctifying and consecrating the whole
world and everything that is in the world, as well as
all the activities that man engages in lawfully in the
world. However, here, just as in the case of man, she
does so, not to perpetuate the sanctified world in its
present condition; she does so to prepare it for becoming the world of the future, the world of the Resurrection. We must look upon the Church not only as the
storehouse of a purifying and redeeming force, but also
as the organism into which God has breathed that force
which brings everything back to Himself and unites
everything in Himself. That is why the Church wants
to take root everywhere: she has to communicate to
everything her redeeming power. Therein is the principle of her catholicity. (We will come back to this
point again). Doubtless, since God has made man free,
she can, and in practice does, meet up with resistance
(though it is impossible in many cases to tell apparent
resistance from real resistance). There are people who
escape her influence, while continuing to use the world
to satisfy their ambitions or their egoism. But wherever
some guilty will does not oppose her, there she spreads
her redeeming power which does its work—visibly or
otherwise.

It is important to have this concept of the Church. Perhaps we picture her to ourselves a little inner circle of souls sheltered in a narrow temple, or we make of her a sect, whereas in reality she is redemption on the march, redemption in action, in the form of a grace not purely invisible, but incorporated into a definite organism. Because she is limited (but here again, let us not forget that she surpasses her visible limits), we think that she herself sets those limits, whereas in fact she never stops unless she runs up against resistance. And she is ever trying to climb over these resisting forces, or rather to disarm them.

It might seem that we have strayed pretty far from the terms we were planning to discuss. In reality, I think I have prepared you to understand them. If indeed we make our own the idea of the Church that I have just outlined, we will see more clearly that she occupies a central place in God's plan, in the "Mystery," as St. Paul says, since this latter consists in the reintegration of fallen humanity in God through Christ. In this plan, The Church is the means and the goal, in her two different and successive (though not strictly distinct), stages. She is the means (of accomplishing this plan) * in her life on earth, and she is the goal of this plan in the life of heaven. There is the provisional stage of the Church—the stage of the present time, the stage in which we know her; and there is her definitive stage. For the Church does not lead men to their end, only to be destroyed herself once this end has been reached. She is not like a tool that we leave behind or break up after we have used it and the work is all done. It is within the Church, reunited in the Church, that we will possess

* Parentheses mine.

God. It is clear that the Church is not only necessary
for the Christian throughout his earthly life, but also
that she is destined to remain forever. The only thing
that will disappear is whatever is demanded by the needs
of the present life, but this same Church which existed
on earth will still exist—though in a transfigured state—
and it will be in her that we will see God. Even now,
there exist a Church militant and a Church triumphant,
which are not two Churches, but one.

The Church is the Climax of Providential Preparations

As the realization of the Divine Plan for the world,
the Church is the culmination of all providential prep-
arations. Since these latter had their visible expression
in the people of Israel, The Church is naturally called—
following St. Paul's lead—the true Israel, the spiritual
Israel, of which the first was but the figure. Since God's
plan consists in the coming of His Kingdom (that is
to say, of a state wherein men, through perfect submission to God, will possess the goods of God Himself,
and will become His heirs not only by promise but by
actual enjoyment), the Church is also called the Kingdom of God. But these two terms are closely related,
because Israel is chosen to become the People of God,
over whom God will reign, and only those who will
agree to live under obedience to God will really and
definitely belong to this people. We shall try to see this
in more detail.

The New Israel

Israel became God's people by a Promise and by a
Covenant. The *promise* is the one God made to Abra-

ham. God promised him that he would have a son of Sara, even though humanly speaking he had reason to despair of that. This son was destined to become the father of a posterity as numerous as the stars, and this posterity would possess the land of Chanaan of which God would dispose to its advantage. This is the sense to be given to the accounts of Genesis which tell us of the promises made to Abraham.

To Moses, God did not make any new promises, but made a pact with him and with the entire people which he represented. God gave His people a Law which it had to keep and which would make of it God's people; in exchange, He Himself would be the protector of His people Israel, He would defend it against its enemies and would assure it the possession of the Promised Land. This pact had a unique character. Although it was made between Israel and God, it did not create the ordinary bonds which are created between the two parties of a contract; but it did establish a unique and mysterious bond. God alone would be Israel's true Teacher, and it is in a very particular sense that the human leaders of this people would govern in the name of God. This is the meaning of "theocracy" in Israel. It was not set up so as to be imitated by the other peoples of the earth, even when they should have become Christian.

It is only in the Church that we find a corresponding arrangement, moved up now, onto a spiritual plane; for that Church remains independent of all temporal power in order to obey a hierarchy which governs her in God's name. This contract between Israel and Yahweh is characterized by the prophets as a betrothal, but despite its religious nature, it still leaves us on the temporal plane: though, in exchange for keeping God's Law, the riches of the Covenant are promised, they are promised to a people which is a natural and earthly reality, to which a man belongs by birth, and they are only material riches at that.

The prophets were to work at spiritualizing these ideas. They were first of all to recall that those who did not keep the Law were excluded from the benefits of the Covenant, that only the "remainder of Israel"— that is, that portion of the people which would remain after Yahweh had eliminated the unworthy—would come into possession of the inheritance. They were to explain that this Law which had to be kept, did not consist of exterior observance, of ceremonies, but rather that it demanded holiness, and that its nature was interior, spiritual, that it called for a disposition of the heart. They did not deny the aspect of material well-being which characterized the state of happiness destined to be the reward of faithfulness, but they stressed that this state had also to be one of justice, of peace, of true holiness. Lastly, here and there this thought is perceived, namely, that though the sinners in Israel are cut off from the inheritance, the just among the other nations could be included in it by their incorporation into the chosen people.

But this first attempt at spiritualizing does not stand out as something final. Jeremias, Ezechiel and Zacharias give presentiments of a new alliance which will surpass the old. Now this new and definitive covenant, sealed with the blood of Christ, will be made with the *Church*. She, then, is the *new Israel*, which follows upon and takes the place of the former Israel. She is a *spiritual Israel*; the goods which come to her as her share of the inheritance no longer consist of land flowing with milk and honey. They are divine goods, eternal life, God Himself. The books of the New Testament multiply expressions which present this characteristic of the Church: *eternal heritage* (Heb., 14:15), *incorruptible heritage* (1 Pet., 2:4), *heritage of the Kingdom of Christ* (Eph., 5:6), *heritage of eternal life* (Tit., 3:7), *access to the city of the living God, the heavenly Jerusalem* (Heb., 12:22), *the city of the saints* (Eph., 2:18-19; Phil., 3:20), *the communication of life with God* (1 Cor., 1:9; 1 John, 1:3).

But no matter how radical this transformation was, the Church did not forget the preparation whose fruit she was. Scarcely had she emerged from the Cenacle where the Spirit had come down, than the Apostles announced to the Jews that the promises made to their fathers had been fulfilled in the completest sense. From here on in, the real Israel existed, the true riches had been given to it. This continuity is noticeable even in the very term which serves to describe this new Israel: *ecclesia* is the Greek word used in the Septuagint versions to translate the Hebrew *Qahal*, which designated the totality of the people of God. The new people follows upon the old; but it has quite different features. It is in no way bound up with natural grouping, nationality, race, etc. Its members are those who are called to it by God, no matter what their origin.

The word *ecclesia* stands out here as a doubly happy choice. On the one hand, it embodies the idea of a call (though this is not the reason the term was chosen); the members of the new people are *the called*, the *Kletoi*. But, on the other hand, we are here dealing with a people, with a related, organized whole, and not with a mere collection of individuals. Undoubtedly, the way in which its unity, and the nature of the bond which united all its members, are to be expressed, will differ according to whether we consider it on earth or in its state of completion in heaven. In one or the other state, however, it remains truly a people, with all that this term indicates as regards the real unity among those who make it up: "We have succeeded (by carrying out the idea of an inheritance promised by God to His people) in knowing that the promises will be fulfilled in a people, a race, and specifically, in understanding why Christians are conscious of being called to salvation in a society, in a Church." (L. Cerfaux, *L'Eglise et le Règne de Dieu*, in "Ephemer. Theol.," Lovan. 1925). It is the Church as a society which acquires the right to inherit the "heavenly goods, the community property which Christians will possess jointly" (ibid., p. 187). This is so much the case that we can say of the Church that she is the organism created to receive the rights to the heavenly inheritance (ibid., p. 91). Without a doubt, it is true that the Christian possesses here below the initial "deposit" of the promised inheritance, and that he will possess it in full some day; but this possession cannot be vested in him as long as he remains in the condition of an isolated individual. He has to enter into God's people, which is organized first according to conditions here on earth, and later on destined to carry on as a heavenly community. Thus, according to the term quoted from Cerfaux, Christians possess the goods of God jointly, not each on his own account and apart from the others. A while back, we were saying, too, that "the Church will see God." Undoubtedly, each individual Christian is destined to see God; by this expression we mean to say that all will not see the same God separately one by one. No, this vision will be common to all, and all will be united in and by the possession of God.

The Church as the Kingdom of God

When we were treating of the earthly Israel, we were talking about a heritage, about goods promised to it. Passing on now to the new Israel, we say that it both possesses now and will possess the good things of God. There is in that an important feature, well-adapted for clarifying the idea of the Church as the Kingdom of God. It is in fact just another way of expressing the Promise, to say that it is the Promise of the possession of the Kingdom. To be in this Kingdom and to take part in it, is, in fact, to possess the divine goods—to possess God. But, the Church is not only the preparation of the Kingdom of God, she is also its realization in practice.

According to one of its aspects, the message of Christ consisted in saying that the Kingdom of God was approaching, that it was imminent. Events disappointed the expectation of those who had seen in that the announcement of the immediate end of the world, and of the imminent establishment of that Kingdom in its definitive state. But Christ had not deceived His hearers. A new state of things has been established, definitive in the sense that there will no longer be any transfer comparable to the transfer from the old to the new alliance; but yet provisional in the sense that what lies hidden in it will be unveiled, and what is possessed in it only in pledge-form and in expectation, will be possessed fully, and from thenceforth with no fear of its being lost. In other words, the Kingdom of God exists in two stages: on earth, in its inchoative fulfillment, and in heaven, in its fulness. However, in both stages this Kingdom is still the Church.

The Church on earth is even now, more than just a promise and a preparation; she begins to be the fulfillment of the Kingdom. We must therefore find a continuity between the Church as she actually exists, and the definitive Kingdom. This continuity consists in the fact that the goods which are to become the lot of the elect exist already in the Church. Using another figure, we can say that the riches of God are the dowry which Christ has brought to His Spouse. Everyone therefore shares in it, in the measure in which he belongs to the Church. Since the principle of the possession of every divine good is the possession of the Spirit, we can understand St. Paul's expression: we possess the "earnest" of the Spirit and not merely the promise of someday having Him. We must in like manner say that the grace which we possess through the Church, is not only a promise of someday possessing divine life in heaven, but is the real possession of this life, though in an imperfect, precarious and obscure way.

We have said that the Church is not only a means, but also an end; not only a way, but a goal. This was done to show that she will not be abolished, but transfigured in the completion which will take place in heaven. We must, however, go further and say that, even in her life on earth, the Church is more than just a means directed to some end, more than a road leading to some destination; she is the inchoative and obscure presence of that which someday is to be perfect and clear. She possesses already, in a mystical manner, the goods of the inheritance and can begin to distribute them. She is the reality of the Kingdom, even now in our midst. We are, therefore, not only supposed to attain the Kingdom in the hereafter, but also to graft ourselves more and more here below onto the Church. The order of the Old Testament was an order of figures—figures of the Church and of heaven. The Church is also a prefiguring of heaven, but she is more besides—she is the order of possession in faith and hope, whereas heaven is the order of perfect and unveiled reality. The relationship between the Church and Heaven, or between the New Testament and its Fulfillment, is not the same as that between the Old Testament and the New, that is, the Church. In the latter, what is one day to be possessed is not only promised and represented, but its substance is already mysteriously present, and it is up to each man to share in it in a more or less real manner, although in the obscurity of faith.

3

The Church: The Body of Christ

What is the sense and bearing of this new expression? What attitude does it require of the Christian with regard to the Church? Those are precisely the questions I would like answered. But beforehand, we have to consider certain difficulties, for that is the only way we will be able to make her (i.e. the Church's) * teachings precise.

Sense and bearing of the expression

Those men who are vivified by Christ, that is, who receive in a continuous flow, through His influence, sanctifying grace, and thereby are united among themselves, those men are in some manner members of Christ, since they share in His life. We have every reason to believe that some of this number do not belong visibly to the Church. Though it is not for us to sound the depth of

* Parenthetical explanation mine.

34

consciences, since that is something God alone can know with absolute certitude, yet we think we have, with regard to this or that individual, moral certitude that he or she has not sinned against the light and is therefore in the grace of God. But it is not this aspect of the question that we will consider today.

Let us consider the Catholic Church. She is visible in her Hierarchy, in her Worship and in her Sacraments, in the members who make her up. Among these members, there are some who do not live by the life of Christ, who are not united to Christ by grace, and are not united to the others by the bond of Charity. There again, without wishing to pass concrete judgment in individual cases and thus usurp God's place, nevertheless we can repeat the declarations that all the Fathers make with anguish of soul: "There is in the Church a mixture of the good and the bad; the net of the miraculous catch, symbolic of the Church, contains all sorts of fish which will be sorted out when the net has been dragged ashore, that is, on the day of the Final Judgment; or again, according to the parable often taken in the same sense, in the field of the householder the weeds are mixed in with the good grain: these weeds are the wicked who here below are members of the Church." Taking a specific case, if a baptized Christian who has the Faith and professes it does not live in conformity with his Faith, he is not living by the life of Christ, because he does not have grace, because he is in the state of sin. Yet he still remains in the Church, he is always part of the Church. It is therefore possible to belong to the Church without really being a member of Christ—at least a living member. Even if the Christian in question is never converted, he will never, for the rest of his life, be able to be less a member of the Church.

It is from this that the temptation arises to separate as being two entities, the Church and the Body of Christ; to put on one side the Body of Christ, this invisible organism, altogether "mystical," the members of which God alone knows, and then on the other side, the visible ecclesiastical organization which permits us to discern easily by means of visible signs, who are or are not its members. This is the position of many Protestants; they say: there are many of these visible organizations. They are legitimate and useful; we must not look down upon the helps they provide. However, none of them is the Body of Christ.

Let us note carefully that even if we were to correct this statement by saying that there is but one legitimate organization, the Catholic Church, we would still not arrive at the doctrine of the Church concerning herself. That is because here, the question is to know just what connection there is between the Church and the Body of Christ. Well, it is rather because the Catholic Church deserves the title of the Body of Christ that she is the only legitimate religious organization. Still, we cannot worm out of the difficulty by saying that all those who are in the Church live by Christ, nor by saying that only those who live by the life of Christ are truly members of the Church, the others being members only in appearance, since it is possible to belong to the Church by Baptism and Faith without belonging to Christ by grace. We cannot say that belonging to the Church by Baptism and belonging to Christ by Faith overlap. The Mystical Christ and the Church-Society are not identical. In what sense therefore are we going to call the

Church the Body of Christ, following the example of Saint Paul and the whole of Christian tradition?

I believe that we are touching the essential point from which all else derives, if we understand that in the order of things chosen by God, the Mystical Christ could not be formed without the visible Church. The reason for this is that Christ has confided His Sacraments to a visible and hierarchical society, the Catholic Church. Obviously it was up to Him to establish the means by which man, once freed from sin, could be united to Himself. But He did not want that to be by means of purely internal acts, nor even by means of rites which each person would perform for and by himself, but rather by the reception of Sacraments of which the Church is the Dispenser. It is by means of Baptism that man is freed from original sin in order to be joined to Christ. It is by means of the Eucharist that his incorporation is completed. (It might even be better to say that the Eucharist, although coming after Baptism, is that which, *par excellence*, brings about incorporation into Christ, since Baptism is oriented toward the Eucharist, and produces its effect only because it involves the desire, at least implicit, for the Eucharist). Those who do not belong visibly to the Church are joined to the Body of Christ only by virtue of a desire for the Sacraments. (Later on, we will speak of the form that this desire can take). But, as a matter of fact, the Sacraments are entrusted to the Catholic Church alone. If in certain cases non-Catholics can confer them validly, it is only on condition that by means of the intention they have of doing what the Church does, they thereby become ministers of the Church as well as of Christ.

The whole of the dogmatic and moral teaching of

the Church, her whole Worship, all her ceremonies, have as their end to dispose people for the fruitful reception of the Sacraments, that they may have the full benefit of the grace which these communicate. Everything in the Church pertaining to the Word or to Worship, has reference to the Sacraments. The Hierarchy, itself basically sacramental, has as its principal *"raison d'être"* the administration of the Sacraments, or the ministry of Word and Worship which prepares souls for their reception. The apostolate—essential to the Church—which she exercises on unbelievers or sinners, has as its end to persuade them to come and draw life from the sacramental fountainheads. . . . It is not simply a matter of convincing someone of a doctrine, but of deciding him to approach the Sacraments with the required dispositions (which obviously include Faith as the first condition of vivification).

Thus we see how, without the visible and hierarchical Church (all of whose members are not necessarily living members of Christ), there is no Mystical Christ living on earth. Just as by means of His Body of flesh, distinct from the Divinity, the Word became in a unique sense present on earth, in Galilee, in the first century of our era, now it is by means of the Church that the Mystical Christ, along with everything that implies in the way of presence and spiritual reality, lives today in the world. This visible society which is the Church is therefore that by which the presence of Christ in His Mystical life is realized here below. That is the reason why the Church can be called the Body of Christ, just as she is, with all her human imperfections.

Let us note, in order to conclude this exposition, that the Sacraments which the Church dispenses are always fertile in her. It is impossible to countenance the hypothesis according to which only those souls not belonging visibly to the Church would be justified (always by means of a desire, at least implicit, for the Sacraments), when in her visible framework every soul would be dead. It is the teaching of the Church that there will always be, in her, souls living by grace, living members of the Mystical Body. Therefore, this prejudice is also incapable of dissociating the Church and the Mystical Body. Perhaps we have to give up all hope of ever having a state of things wherein all the visible members of the Church will live, and live especially in a *full* manner, by the life of Christ. At least, the Church will always bear this life in herself. But, on the other hand, we are equally unable to think that she will someday disappear totally as a visible organization, as long as the world lasts, because, just like a soul no longer joined to the world by its body, Christ would thereby lose all point of contact, so to speak, with the world He must continue to save.

The Church is therefore the visible organism by means of which Christ lives and acts in this world. The presence and the action of Christ in this world are never without some reference to the Sacraments which He instituted, which He entrusted to the Church whose whole activity, in turn, centers on their administration. This presence and action, therefore, never lack some connection with the Church. Whatever in her is of divine institution was chosen by Christ as a means of expressing and realizing this life which He wants for our souls, and by that, of accomplishing the total recovery of the universe which has to be brought back to God. *It is because of this relationship, established by*

Christ Himself, between the visible Church and the life which He continues in our midst, that she deserves to be called the Body of Christ, despite the fact that all of those who are in her bosom are not living members of Christ, and despite the fact that there can be many things more or less open to criticism, many weak or ill-suited features, in the complex accessory machinery which has been added on to what in her is of divine origin.

I believe that it was necessary to go into these particulars so as not to allow the bond between Christ and the Church to be broken or loosened, while, however, not calling identical things which must be kept distinct, without confusing, as one Protestant accused Catholicism of doing, "Papal establishment with the Kingdom of God."

Attitude of the Christian toward the Church, the Body of Christ

These clarifications are fruitful insofar as they help us to understand what our own attitude must be. They justify what we have said about the demands which the Church makes as regards the place she wants to hold in the life of the faithful. As Saint Augustine used to say to the Christians of Hippo: "A member cannot live by the spirit which animates the body unless it remain united with the body; if therefore you wish to live by the Spirit of Christ, remain in the Body of Christ." Whoever wants to live by Christ must set at the very basis of his religious life, the doctrines concerning God, Christ, the world, oneself, which are professed by the Church. He must seek a means of union with Christ not in actions he himself chooses, but in the Sacraments of the Church. He must walk toward God by the paths which the Church traces for him. It is by introducing one's activity into the framework set up by the Church that one succeeds in being penetrated by Christ.

But there is another aspect of this submission to the Church which has to be considered, another aspect which is not always sufficiently brought to light. Everything in the Church is designed to permit union with Christ. Her visible element—and by that I understand equally the formulas of Faith which she defines, and her Hierarchy and Worship—does not have its *"raison d'être"* in itself. The visible Church is, we might say, the Sacrament of Christ. She makes sense only in that way. If she gives us an order, if she takes us into herself, it is not in order to domineer over us, but rather to hand us over to Christ. If the Catholic is the subject of a Power, it is in order to become the member of a Body. "His juridical dependence on the former has as its purpose his vital insertion into the latter. Nor is his submission a resignation. He does not have merely the duty of obeying orders or of showing deference to counsels; he has to participate in a life, communicate in a spirit." (H. de Lubac, *Catholicism*).

This life, this spirit, are the Life and Spirit of Christ. We can therefore say of the Church what is said of God: "To serve the Church is to reign" (*servire Ecclesiae regnare est*). For obedience to the Church, intellectual obedience in matters of Faith as well as obedience to the Commandments, will succeed in pulling us out of our ignorance (religious ignorance, we mean), from our egoism, from the servitude of the flesh, in order to bring us to the liberty of the Spirit: *Ubi Spiritus Domini, ibi libertas* (where the Spirit of the Lord is, there also is liberty).* In fact, it is when we live by Christ and are led by Him, that we are really ourselves. It is then that we are re-established in the truth of our being. It is then that we do what we wish in the very depths of our own being, instead of following the impulses of that part of us which is not really our being, but only its corruption and degradation. It is clear that the Christian who contents himself with fulfilling, even fulfilling punctually, his obligations toward the Church, does not grasp the profound sense of his duty; he keeps the letter, but fails to attain to the spirit. He does not know why he is obeying.

And so it is that his obedience is for him somewhat of a burden. We have to see in our obedience the instrument of our own true liberation. It is the means by which we are placed under the leadership of Christ, a leadership which, however, is not exercised over us from the outside; rather, it renews from within our ways of thinking and of willing. Under these conditions the yoke of Christ is not heavy, because it makes us love that which it imposes. But the only way to this kind of liberation is submission to the Church of Christ.

It can happen that a believing Christian—this follows from what we have just seen—will be unjustly suspected by other Christians, not only those who are such merely in name, but by real Christians, because they are not wholly protected from human limitations and imperfections. It can happen that he is treated too harshly, even unjustly condemned, by the Hierarchy—history gives some indisputable cases of this. For, while the assistance of the Holy Spirit sees to it that the Church cannot teach an erroneous doctrine in matters of Faith

* Translation not in French text.

or Morals, when she speaks with all her authority, and while we are also assured that by her conduct and her decisions she will never compromise irremediably the progress of the Kingdom of God in this world, nevertheless the fact remains that the men who exercise this authority in the Church are not thereby preserved from all error, from all weakness, from every danger of abusing their authority. This is so true that those who are subject to them can suffer unjustly.

There are two ways in which the Christian can suffer at the hands of the Church. He can suffer because of what is divine in her, because of actions by which the Hierarchy rightly carries out its mission of speaking in the name of God. This is because the Divine Truth, the manifestation of the divine exigencies, is fatal to the dregs of egotism and imperfection which remain in the Christian. But he can also suffer as a result of what remains human, "too human," in the Church, on the part of those who exercise some portion of her authority. If the latter were more perfect, this suffering would be spared him. He can, therefore, find that he is balked in the most just of aspirations. Let us not be afraid to say that, were it only to forestall that idea that we base our absolute fidelity to the Church on a refusal to face incontestable evidence. Nothing is more to be feared than letting such a conviction grow among those on the outside. But, even in such a case, even if he were to be deeply wounded, the Christian does not even raise the question of leaving the Church or of bargaining his submission, and, while he has the right to make just claims, he does not let himself stoop to bitter recrimination. He knows that by leaving the Church he would be losing the life of Christ. He knows that by showing disrespect to those who, despite possible errors or faults even, remain the dispensers of authority, he would be acting contrary to the impulses of the Spirit of Christ.

The Church remains for him the one who, by her teaching and by her Sacraments, gives him Christ, the one who alone can give him Christ. What sort of proportion is there between what he suffers at her hands—which he would not suffer if she were perfect—and what she gives him? There is between the two all the difference between suffering, deep perhaps but passing, and a gift of infinite value: participation in Christ, and through Him in all the divine riches. He knows moreover that the Church, in spite of the gropings of the men who govern her, will never compromise irremediably the destinies of the Kingdom of God, as we have said, and he knows that no other society but the Church can fulfill these efficaciously. If, like every true Christian, he is intent on the progress of the Kingdom of God, on the growth of the Mystical Body, and not on the satisfaction of his personal grudges, he will never seek to set up another "church" in opposition to the Church of Christ. History paints for us the picture of men who, after being condemned by the Church, and that often justly, have revolted against her. Let us not pass upon them a judgment God has reserved for Himself. We cannot measure the part illusion played in directing their conduct, nor the degree of guilt present in these illusions. But we do say that their conduct is in itself damnable and could never be taken as a model. We are merely pointing out what is to be the rule of our own conduct.

You can see that there is no need of closing our eyes to any of the facts which are contained in the History of the Church. But surely it is not an easy task to make those who do not share our Faith understand this attitude. Precisely because they see in the Church only her external social reality and her human elements, they draw up a "balance sheet" of what, in certain circumstances, the Christian suffers at the hands of the Church, and of what he receives from her—not on the material plane but better, on the visible plane—and they are tempted to conclude that this balance sheet is, in certain cases, heavy on the debit side. They fail to see everything the Christian receives in the order of invisible things, the insertion into the life of Christ which tears him away from his sin and from everything in himself which tends to degrade him, to shrivel or stop him up altogether.

This idea of the Church as the Body of Christ is one of the reasons which explain the importance placed upon her unity, her visible unity. It is because there is but one Body of Christ that there must be only one Church— one Mystical Body, all of whose members live by the same life, but just as much also a single visible Body which is not numerically one with the other, but constitutes for that other the means of realization and expression. The unity of the religious society is not an arbitrary fact. If the Church were a human institution, a result of the coming together of Christians desirous of giving one another mutual help in their religious lives, it might be possible to admit that these Christians would group themselves according to affinities of all sorts. But if Christ has chosen a Body, if He has willed to entrust to a visible organism the Sacraments which communicate life, it follows that no other church can be founded alongside of His Church. Certainly, it is always possible to work to better her in her human elements, but it would be futile to seek to change her or replace her with something better, or despairing of her, to try to create outside of her a religious organization, to gather up the heritage she would have allowed to fall. That would be a huge illusion.

The decisive question is this: is it the believers who, on their own initiative, have grouped themselves into a "church," or is it Christ Who, by entrusting His teachings and His Sacraments to a Church, has thereby chosen a Body by means of which He will live and pour out His life? In the first hypothesis it is difficult to see, actually, why there would not be many religious organizations, each with its advantages and disadvantages, its strong and its weak points. It is equally difficult to see how these would be exempt from the law of time, from sclerosis or corruption; how their adherents, seeing that they have become unequal to their task, would be wrong in quitting them some day or dissolving them to found others more alive and better adapted. But, in the second hypothesis, there can never be but one Church, the one which Christ chose as His Body. There can therefore be no reason for leaving her to organize a new one, because a new one would be incapable of transmitting the life of Christ. At the same time, we cannot say that Christ will ever allow the Body He has chosen and which is vivified by His Spirit, to fall into a state of decay. And so, while it may be possible to re-form the Church (it can be said that this task, though more urgent at certain times, is always necessary), yet it can never be possible to transform or replace her.

Now we are able to understand the beautiful words of Bossuet which are often repeated: The Church is

Jesus Christ poured out and communicated. This statement does not imply a failure to recognize what is imperfect and human in the Church—as though the idea were to say that throughout the ages she has never presented to the eyes of men anything which was not perfectly worthy of Christ. But she is a visible organism which not only is in possession of the correct notion of Christ and preserves His doctrine intact, but also, by means of her sacraments, communicates His life. It is to Christ that she joins those whom she admits to membership. And we are sure that she will never fail in her task. She is the mediatrix by whom Jesus, through the ages, acts on men in order to gather them together, making them "one" with Himself. In order, therefore, to underline this characteristic of the active presence of Christ through the Church and her Sacraments, we can say that the Church is Jesus Christ pouring Himself out and communicating Himself.

We will conclude on a point which will permit us to bring into focus a question often touched upon. As we have said, everything in the Church is directed to her work of communicating Christ; everything aims at the formation and growth of the Mystical Body. Whatever in her makeup comes from Christ is perfectly adapted to this end. Whatever men add on to that, as well as the manner in which they utilize the powers they have received, all that has to be directed to the same end. It is possible to belong to the Church without being vivified by Christ, but actually one belongs to the Church only in order that he may be vivified by Christ. It is perhaps because we have not given sufficient reflection to this truth that we are sometimes taken aback by the presence within the Church of non-vivified Christians. We imagine that everybody belongs in the same degree to the Church, as if membership required mere inscription on a register! Either we are registered or we are not; there is no middle course.

But let us think rather in terms of those groups—such as the family, where a common spirit, a common life, has to be developed. True, we belong to these, and in a real sense, by the mere fact, for example, of birth. But our belonging is more or less profound in the degree that we live by its spirit or remain a stranger to it. The Christian who in the Church lives by Christ, belongs more profoundly to the Church than the one who does not live by Christ. His belonging is, if we may say so, more complete because it attains its true end. The one who believes without living in a Christian manner is not by that fact outside the Church, for he is not wholly a stranger to Christ; for on the one hand, Faith is always a grace from Christ which enlightens the understanding, and on the other hand, it always presupposes adherence of the will. Now this act of the will is imperfect because it does not go far enough as to make the person faithful to the Commandments, and the grace of Faith does not then have its normal prolongation. But such a Christian is not totally removed from the influence of Christ, and the Faith he professes constitutes the first and indispensable basis for recovering normal relations. Nevertheless, his membership in the Church, while real, is precarious. Either he will grow up some day to a living Faith proved by works, or else, if death finds him in this state, he will not pass into the Church Triumphant, but will be left outside. He does not belong to the Eternal Church, the Church which, through purified eyes, will see God eternally.

You see therefore how provisional is the membership in the Church of a sinful believer. Either he will cease being a sinner, or he will be rejected from the Church when she is wholly spotless. The Church is not *in aeternum* a mixture of good grain and weeds, of just and unjust members. She is on the way to that definitive state where whatever is mortal in her will be consumed, that is, where everything pertaining to the conditions of her earthly existence will have disappeared. It is toward this future condition, toward this fulness and this purity that Saint Augustine, for instance, loved to turn his eyes. We must imitate him if we wish to understand all the grandeur which the Church hides and prepares, that Church which lives before our eyes and in which we live.

4

Interior Life of the Church

What we are to understand by this expression

If it is true that the Church is not merely a visible reality, a grand sociological fact, but also a spiritual and supernatural reality, then she possesses what we must call an interior life, taking that expression in the sense that Christianity has given it. We are not to see in it only a term used to designate and as it were to synthesize the interior life of each individual Christian, or even the extra impetus which would result from such synthesis. If it is true that the Church is the mother of Christians, that a man becomes a Christian only by participating in the Church, then the interior life of the Christian is a sharing in that of the Church.

Here we run up against this same fundamental truth, namely that it is not a question of Christians uniting to form the Church, but of the Church forming Christians. If we do not wish to disfigure the Church, we must not consider her solely in the light of the categories which serve in the case of societies of human origin. The concept of a society which is not produced by the members who make it up, is certainly a bit disconcerting. In the way we propound it, it would be absurd, if the Church were not something other than what we are able to see in her.

But, as we have said, the Church is a mystery. We do not know her in her entirety when we know, even perfectly, her organization. She possesses a type of activity we may call exterior because those outside the fold can see its effects: the ministry of the Word, worship, the apostolate, works of charity, social influence. This exterior activity, however, is essentially related to her interior life. It has value only because it proceeds from the latter, and introduces one into it. We cannot repeat often enough, if we wish to correct certain spontaneous but deceiving viewpoints: whatever is visible in the Church has for its essential purpose to procure an ever-expanding and ever-deepening participation in her interior life. Outside of this perspective, we would be incapable of understanding the Church. Moreover, a Christian gives full meaning to his own belonging to the Church only when he opens himself up to this interior life, and allows himself to be more and more deeply penetrated by it.

Characteristics of the Interior Life of the Church

In order to understand what this interior life is, we must approach it successively and from different angles. In this way only will we see it in all its richness. That is what we are going to try to do.

1) First of all, this interior life takes on in each per-

son a personal character. The Church in no way aims
to draw her faithful into a sort of blind collective impetus wherein each loses his personality, exists only as a
member of the group, does not think, does not express
himself on his own, but is as it were imbued with an external force. Romano Guardini has pointed out the
calm, reasonable nature of Catholic Liturgy. Even here,
when they are united to pray in common, the faithful
keep their individuality; they observe a certain order
among themselves, are united, but not fused, and the
same formulas can and must have a particular resonance
on the lips of each one. The Church does not have recourse to methods of suggestion to impose her life upon
us. On the contrary—and this is possible for her because
she is not merely an external society—it is from within
that she draws out our prayer-life. She makes it spring
forth from our deepest self, as a living activity. This
activity, moreover, blossoms out according to the temperament, the psychology, the character, of each one,
whence comes the admirable diversity of Catholic
prayer. It is in the saints, whose wealth it exhausted,
so to speak, that we must admire its full flowering.

After having drawn out our prayer-life, the Church
continues to guide it, for we could give a false orientation to this impetus received from her. The prayer-forms
to which she has given her approval are thus so many
props for it, so many pure sources where we may nourish it. We cannot understand the role of these prayer-
forms if we separate them from this life-surge which the
Church has communicated to us. At once a spiritual
reality and a visible organization, she acts in us from
within and from without at one and the same time . . .
from within by the influence of a life which uplifts us,

utilizing in the process whatever is good in us, and from the outside by forms and formulas which uphold and orientate this impetus.

I have spoken chiefly of prayer because it is there that the basis of our interior life finds expression, it is that which reveals this interior life most accurately. But the same holds true whatever the aspect under which we consider this interior life. It is a communication of the Church in us, and is nonetheless altogether personal, for it rises up in us and bears the traces of what we ourselves are. And it is all the more personal, the more deeply rooted it is in the Church.

2) But, at the same time, the interior life communicated by the Church is a *life of communion*. Even though communal prayer takes on in each of us a personal character, yet the private prayer of the Christian, even if it is made in secret, is never an isolated prayer—his interior life is never the life of a solitary being. He always leads it in real communion with his fellows.

This stands out in the religious act *par excellence*, the Mass. Here, it is the Church which offers herself to God, it is the assembly of the faithful, the Christian people, and not a number of individuals. The whole Church unites herself to the sacrifice of Christ in order to be united to His Resurrection and His life in the Spirit. The priest at the altar does not speak in his own name, nor in the name of one of the faithful or of a group of the faithful, but in the name of the whole Church, in the name of all those who by their interior attitude, do not refuse to ratify her offering. Those who assist are not there each for himself—it is the whole community which offers itself with Christ. This truth is very admirably symbolized by the custom which is spreading today, of

answering the priest in common. But those who assist
must not forget their link with the rest of the Church.
To prevent that from happening, it is sufficient to be
attentive to the Church's prayers themselves. Even when
he prays for himself, a Christian knows that he is pray-
ing for a member of the Church—so that this member
might keep the place assigned to it in the Body, and by
that fact all the other members are bystanders to his
prayer.

This communion in prayer is a manifestation of communion in the Christian life itself. One of the articles of
our Creed is that concerning the Communion of Saints.
It has often been asked if, in the original formula, the
word "sanctorum" were in the neuter and ought to be
understood as "communication in (the) holy things,"
or in the masculine, in which case it would designate
"the communion of Christians among themselves."
Without going into the discussion, let us say simply that
both senses are true and at one and the same time.
Christians participate in holy things—all the realities
which the Church possesses in a mysterious manner, and
which culminate in the Eucharist. They participate
therein together, in common. Contrary to material possession, this sort of possession unites, for one cannot
benefit from it apart from the others. But there is also
(thanks above all to the Eucharist) a communion of
Christians in virtue of which what one does has value
also for the others. This communion, moreover, extends
from the faithful who live here below to those who are
undergoing a final purification, or who are in glory. Of
this fact, the prayers of the Mass give striking testimony.

We cannot expand on this subject, even to point out

the misunderstandings of the dogma, the deformations it has undergone, sometimes from within the Church as well as from outside. Let us say merely that this communion does not take away any portion of personal liberty and personal responsibility. The merits of others dispense no one from putting out the effort required of him, nor do they permit him to save and sanctify himself without hurting himself a little. Such a representation of the matter is but a caricature.

We must rather understand it in the sense that these merits, by the mediation of grace, which produced them originally, will draw out and prop up our own efforts. Nothing can dispense anyone from giving himself to God by an act which must be free. But to have the courage to perform this act, and perform it ever better and better, we can count on the prayers and virtues of our fellows, which will win us the needed grace. This grace will not replace our liberty, but will stimulate it. Everybody can always be obstinate in refusing and resisting this influence which seeks to uplift him. But if despite everything, we struggle on toward the good, then, no matter how much we grope and fail, we can count on the explicit prayers of our brethren, or on those implicit prayers which are their acts of virtue, to win us the grace we call for. Likewise, every generous thing we do becomes for them a source of grace, whether it serves to stir them up in their inertia, or to help them in their march toward perfection. And all of us together lean for support on the prayers of the Church in heaven.

And so you have the twofold characteristic of this interior life of the Church. On one hand, it is lived in a personal manner by every Christian, but at the same time it is a commuion of all in the same spiritual goods, and a mutual support in the struggle to possess these more fully. It is a community of life—not in the trite sense of common habits and conduct, but in the sense that there is in all one same principle of life—a profound communion that must find expression in prayer wherein everyone is concerned with everyone else, and in fraternal aid each time the occasion presents itself. Representing the Church as a Body shows quite well that each Christian as a member of this Body plays a necessary part. But it also follows that each must support the others in their own action, and it is in the degree that he does this that each truly lives by the life of the Church.

3) The two characteristics which we have just considered flow from the very nature of this interior life. We will see more clearly the latter's "raison d'être" when we have penetrated more deeply into its nature.

Let us say at the outset that it is a *divinized life*. That is to say, it not only makes us direct our thoughts and our actions toward objects of a different sort, but it makes us perform acts through which we participate in God. It is essentially a life of Faith, Hope and Charity— that is the focal point for everything else. What Faith gives us is the ability to think like God about God Himself, about ourselves, about the world. It substitutes God's point of view for our personal point of view. Too often, we consider Faith only in its painful and imperfect aspects, those by which it is opposed to full vision. But we must not forget the positive features it gives us: it makes us see the world and its history and makes us evaluate everything from God's point of view—that is to say, truthfully. It keeps us from basing ourselves on illusory values in leading our lives. To live the life of Faith is to see whatever is related to our spiritual life and the spiritual life of mankind through God's eyes. It is, therefore, a question of much more than just adding a certain number of truths to the list of those we already know.

As for Charity, that consists in loving God, the world, others and ourselves, with a love which is a participation in God's love. It transforms, in order to divinize, our natural manner of loving.

By Hope, finally, we desire, we await, for enjoyment in the life hereafter, the possession of the only good which can attract the one whose thoughts are God's thoughts. It is not the expectation of happiness such as one who considers the satisfaction of egoism as a good can desire, for God does not think that the satisfaction of egoism, even in the hereafter, is a good.

You see now what this life consists in, this life which the Church possesses and communicates to her children in the measure in which they consent to be enriched (though to receive this enriching, one has to let himself be stripped of whatever is the object of spontaneous desire). It is a wholly external viewpoint to think merely that the Church imposes truths to be accepted, and orders to be executed. She renews us interiorly, she transforms us, for she renders us capable of a knowledge and a love whose principle is divine, and which remain inaccessible to those who reject her. The life which flows in the Church is truly a divine life.

And so we are constantly brought back to that concept of a reality present in the Church which is altogether different from its social and visible organization, and which the latter must serve. If we deny one or the other of these two factors, we cause the Church to van-

ish. She exists only by their union. Without visible organization, the divine life no longer is introduced into
the world to take possession of men. Without divine life,
the Church would be, so to speak, only a corpse. That,
however, is precisely to what she is reduced by some
men who imagine they know her.

4) Let us try to penetrate a bit deeper into the nature
of this divine life, by considering the source from which
it emanates. It proceeds from the Father, from whom
everything comes. He gives it to us through His Son
Jesus Christ, who is, as St. Paul tells us, the Head of the
Body; but Christ in turn communicates it to us through
the spirit. According to the teaching common to both
St. Paul and St. John—a teaching which they set forth
each from his own point of view—the glorified Christ
acts by the Spirit who is sent at once by the Father and
the Son. Moreover, the Fathers often say that the Holy
Spirit is the soul of the Church. He is the principle of
her life. Naturally, He is not the instrument of the Son
in a sense which would involve real subordination, nor
in a sense excluding direct contact between the faithful
and Christ. With the Spirit, or "in the Spirit," to use the
traditional phrase, we possess the Son, we are united to
the Son, just as by the Son we are united to the Father—
or, to use the language of St. John, just as by dwelling
in the Son we dwell in the Father.

Last year, while speaking of the role of Christ as Mediator, we pointed out the fact of going through Christ
does not create a gap between us and the Father. Given
the reciprocal immanence of the Divine Persons (we
must here get rid of any spatial images), union with one
brings about union with the others. But there is nonetheless an order which corresponds to the very order of

the Persons within the Trinity. "When God wants to sanctify souls, He sends His well-beloved Son, the universal mediator of grace; and the Son in turn, in conjunction with His Father, sends the Spirit of holiness. The sanctifying action, therefore, takes place according to the order of the eternal Processions." (Prat—Theology of St. Paul).

It is therefore the Trinity which is at work in the Church. It is from the Trinity that the interior life of the Church flows: *Ecclesia de Trinitate*. We can say that the Church is the place wherein the Eternal Plan of Love of the Trinity is accomplished. This Plan is in fact to remake humanity to Its image. The Trinity is three distinct Persons in the one God, Father, Son, and Spirit, whose bond is love. Mankind will therefore be in Its image if it is unified, while maintaining personal distinction, by a love which is a participation in that Love with which the Divine Persons love each other eternally.

We do not know which part of our humanity, yielding to the attractions of Divine Love, will let itself be refashioned in the image of the Trinity. That is a question we are not for the moment expected to go into. But we must understand clearly that what is going on in the Church and by the Church, is precisely this participation in the life of the Trinity—a life lived even on earth, let us not forget, by beings who have to tear themselves progressively away from evil, and repair their past.

Now we see more clearly why the Christian life is a life a communion. This communion is not something accessory or superadded. If it is true that the source of the life communicated by the Church is in the Trinity, then she cannot do otherwise than reunite and reassemble those who at first were divided amongst themselves by indifference or hostility. A person could not receive this life and remain in his "shell." The Trinity is a mystery of love and unity—how is it possible to resemble It, better, live by Its life, without tending to unity?

There, moreover, we have the deepest reason for the Church's unity, unity which flows upon and is the expression of her interior life. There is only one Body of Christ, which communicates to its members a life which can only be lived in union with the other members, a life which is in itself a reconciling and cohesive force. We cannot live such a life apart, or in isolated, separate groups. Doubtless, this unity is compatible with all sorts of differences, whether individual or collective. For example, in the Catholic Church, there are different rites, and in the Latin rite alone a great deal of diversity again. But it is not compatible with schism. That has always been considered a fault, the great fault against Charity. "*Ut unum sint, sicut ego et tu, Pater, unum sumus.*" The unity of the Father and the Son does not prevent their being personally distinct. Likewise, the unity of the Church is not without its divergencies, but what is unacceptable is rupture of the communion. Visible unity is the consequence and the expression, as well as the means, of interior unity based on love. The interior life which the Church communicates to her children is communion with God, but also the communion of men amongst themselves.

The Church believes that this life is the only factor making for the true unity of mankind. Let us consider the contrast between the scene of Babel and that of

Pentecost. At Babel, there is an attempt at union without and against God, which ends up in the division caused by the confounding of languages. At Pentecost, the Apostles are understood by everyone in his own tongue —no unification, no suppression of enriching differences, but a union which rises above and harmonizes them. (This does not exclude mankind from creating institutions to favor and seal unity on the earthly plane. But these will attain their end only if they are born of the Christian spirit, if Christian love has inspired them and continues to support them. Without this they will collapse or become fresh occasions of discord).

The Church is, in short, a community of love. That is the culminating point of her interior life. Those who belong to her without being made part of this community of love do not attain the purpose of their incorporation. This love does not spring forth on the human plane—it comes from the Trinity Itself. In her visible organization, by her sacraments, rich in spiritual efficacy, the Church is the implanting on earth of the unifying love by which the Trinity lives. In her, this love comes down to earth into the midst of a mankind whose members are isolated, opposed, in order to reconcile them to each other by bringing them back to God. She contains the divine strength, the only force capable of reassembling the great fold of humankind.

This interior life of the Church deserves its name, because its principle is within the Church, and because it is a force which introduces itself within each life. But it is manifest on the outside in all types of institutions, in living habits, etc. Nor is it for some purely human success, for some realization which would take place on earth and pass away with the earth, that the Church thus reassembles men—even less is it for her own advantage, for purposes of domination or influence. It is in order to bring them to that definitive state where, fully united, they will live in common by the life of the Trinity.

5

The Catholicity of the Church

Meaning of the term

One of the most popular appellations of the Church is that of "catholic." It is in a letter addressed to the people of Smyrna by Saint Ignatius of Antioch, who died a martyr around the year 107, that we find the first mention of the adjective *Katholikè* used of the Church. Toward the third century, and no doubt up to the seventh, this word was often used as a substantive; the "catholica" is one of St. Augustine's favorite ways of designating the Church.

I hardly need to recall to you that the word itself signifies "universal." But what happens is that when we speak of the "Catholic Church," we thereby understand one Church among others; the term "catholic" serves to distinguish her from the others, to contrast her to the others. We therefore use it in a restrictive sense; the Catholic Church—not only in the eyes of those who are strangers to her, but even in the eyes of many of her children—is this determinate religious organization which leaves out a considerable mass of men; it is a partial reality with restricted frontiers. This is a usage imposed by historical misfortunes, but it is also a viewpoint in itself too narrow. If indeed (and unfortunately so) in the eyes of one who sees only the visible element of the Church in her present state, this is an incontestable fact, the very title of "catholic" claimed by the Church constitutes a permanent protest against this same fact. It affirms that this is not a *de jure* situation, and what is more, that it is true even *de facto* only with regard to the visible aspect of the matter, that is, if one neglects to consider the interior dynamism which animates the Church, the invisible reality which explains her.

By calling herself Catholic, the Church proclaims that she does not accept the existing situation as definitive, that she is making an effort to change it, and that everyone of her members has the duty of working at that along with her. To say that the Church is Catholic is to say that she is universal by her very essence, that the life she gives tends to universal diffusion, that she is intended for the whole of mankind, and that as a consequence, as long as she is not co-extensive with mankind, she will strive to go beyond what she has already accomplished in order to win over what still remains estranged from her. I do not wish to say that she will someday reach that point; we must always take into account human liberty which can say no. But it is essential for her to tend thereto, and this is so not in virtue of a mere external mandate, an external obligation imposed on her, but in virtue of the very nature of the life which animates her. For her, that is a "natural" activity, an activity which necessarily follows from what she is.

The Catholicity of the Church, an intrinsic characteristic

Sometimes people want to make this catholicity out to be something we can appreciate in a material way. It would thus consist in the fact that the Church has adherents over the whole surface of the globe, in the most diverse of countries and in every civilization, so that she possesses samples of mankind in its entirety. (These people also add, by way of subsidiary consideration, the large number of her adherents). This is not the place to set forth the reasons which have led to this way of presenting things. Let us say merely that such a conception results above all from a concern for apologetics rather than from doctrinal considerations. It is an endeavor to bring out a striking mark of the true Church, rather than to know her nature. Therefore, if this idea is held to, it results in a restriction of the notion of catholicity, and that, on top of everything else, compromises the very argument sought from it. It is correct to point out the expansion of the Church; that fact is suitable for presenting the problem to a mind which is searching, for it is in fact an extraordinary thing, this co-habitation in the Church of men so different in their civilization, their culture, their customs, who nevertheless accept the same Faith, the same Sacraments, the same authority. It would be vain to seek an explanation of this outside of the divine nature of the Church. It nevertheless remains that this universal diffusion is a manifestation of the catholicity of the Church, and not catholicity itself.

It even happens that the value of such a manifestation

is restricted too much by insisting above all upon the number of the faithful and the fact of their presence in every land, rather than on the diversity of the members of the Church. But, even when one knows how to bring out its bearing, he must not take this manifestation for the quality of which it is a part expression, or which is guessed at through its means. The work of the artist permits us to discover his talent, but not to exhaust all knowledge of it—it is a fruit of his genius, not the genius itself. In like manner, catholicity is not primarily a fulfillment of the Church, a fact in itself visible, but rather an intrinsic quality. We can find traces of this quality in facts, but we get the full notion of it only through Faith. "The Church was already Catholic on Pentecost morning, when all her members were gathered in a small room. She was Catholic when the waves of Arianism seemed to submerge her. She would still be Catholic if tomorrow mass apostasy made her lose most of her adherents. In essence, Catholicity is not a matter of geography or of numbers. If it is true that it must expand in space and manifest itself in time before the eyes of all, it is, for all that, not of a material but of a spiritual nature. It is, as a matter of fact, something intrinsic to the Church." (H. de Lubac, *Catholicism*).

What this characteristic consists in

The Catholic character of the Church consists in this, that the life she brings and communicates is of such a nature as to be capable of assembling the whole of humankind and bringing all of it back to God. Such is her capacity, and such is her vocation. That holds true for every civilization, from the richest and most refined to those we call primitive, those which are given to action as well as those which tend rather to meditation. Within each civilization, the same thing holds true for all the degrees of personal culture, for all states of life, for all ages and all conditions. And all of that is true not only in the sense that in each of these categories the Church would find souls to bring to God—of course, there is no one who cannot find his place in the Church, no one who need feel himself a stranger to her; but we must say more. The Church can accept, in order to transform and impart eternal value to, whatever is human in each one. She does not limit herself to adding a religious life to the life we call human, but she gives a religious meaning to that human life—to the life of thought, to family life, to manual labor, to the struggle for the progress and transformation of the world. In that way she is capable of drawing our whole material universe into her movement toward God.

We are frightened, and rightly so, by the way mankind uses the mastery it has acquired over the world. But we must not look upon that as a catastrophe, as though the progress of science and technology had unleashed evil forces. The evil is in man who removes himself from the influence of God and from the divine activity in the Church. But, in the measure in which mankind consents to live by her, the Church can transform its activity to the point of making it the expression of Charity. She is thus able to reach every man, and everything that there is in each man.

But, in order to have a complete notion of catholicity, we must add one more important note: by means of the common life she transmits to each the Church is capable of uniting in one whole these men who are so different one from another. She can cause an immense current of spiritual "give and take" to circulate among them. In short, she can make them live this life of communion we were talking about the other day. To say that there is not a single man she cannot vivify is to say that there is not a single man she is unable to bring into this communion. The catholicity of the Church is not only the power of reaching all the individuals which make up mankind, but the power of making of them a whole, a real unity—the Mystical Body of Christ. Thus Catholicism reveals to men their unity, and at the same time, the source of this unity and the means to achieve it.

If the Church is able to address herself to all men and assemble them all, it is because she touches upon something which exists in all and is common to them all. She herself, as we have said, brings the life of the Trinity. And that is something which, consciously or not, every man needs, and of which every man is "capable." The whole of mankind is created in the image of the Trinity. Every man, without knowing it, bears the mark of that in his inmost being. It is not a feature which depends upon time, upon places, civilizations, or individual conditions. It is not something which some can acquire and others not. Man cannot do otherwise than live according to this image. Its acquisition or abolition does not depend on him.

The movement which results from that fact is beyond coercion—it is the spiritual dynamism which animates humanity. People can pervert it, but they cannot suppress or choke it. When a man fails to orient it toward its true end, he will necessarily seek illusory satisfactions for it, the saddest of which is the infinite search for pleasure. Man's insatiability in search of pleasure, even as it disgusts him, bears witness to the nobility of his nature. Only a being made for what surpasses all measure can thus seek without limit sensible satisfactions. With others, the need for God tries to find a substitute in a mysticism of purely human content. But the need exists for everybody. There is therefore not a single man for whom the Church's message is not meant.

There is another aspect which we cannot neglect if we wish to understand completely the catholicity of the Church. These men who are all basically identical to one another insofar as they are images of the Trinity, are nonetheless really diverse. I do not speak here of contrasts, which are always odious, or of artificial differences which follow upon certain fashions. There are among men normal and beneficent differences which make them complement one another. Human values are divided up among peoples, civilizations, individuals, in such a way that mankind is not made up of interchangeable parts, so to speak, but of personalities and groups capable of mutually enriching one another. Could the catholicity of the Church consist only in a unity more profound than these differences? Could the Church merely say to us: "Underneath, or beyond, all that separates you, there is something which can unite you. That is the only thing that interests me, and I need not concern myself with the rest?"

The question could be put another way, if we started with a fact: the Church adapts herself to times and places. Alongside the universal and permanent elements in what she offers us, what she requires of everybody in the way of doctrine or practice, she also accepts, when it comes to expressing the religious life, differences which are considerable. It is pointless to list them; you can uncover by yourselves numerous examples. It is enough to have travelled from one country to another, or to have studied a bit of History, or just to have looked around us, to realize that lives lived not more or less on the fringes of the Church but wholly in her, and under her influence, present divergencies worthy of note.

How are we to interpret this attitude of the Church? Is it a policy, not, doubtless, with selfish ends, but with a view to facilitating the penetration of Christianity among all peoples and civilizations? Such a policy would not, in itself, be blameworthy, since it takes nothing away from the message of Christ, and does not flatter anyone for what is culpable or less good. It is a legitimate and wise procedure not to disturb natural or acquired differences which do not compromise the Christian life. There is indeed something of that idea in the attitude of the Church. If she refuses to cover up the requirements of the Gospel, she refuses just as much to load the faithful down with unnecessary burdens. This we see right from the beginnings of her History. At Jerusalem, the Apostles, reunited to solve the problems arising out of the entrance into the Church of pagans who did not pass first through Judaism, set up this rule: *"It has seemed good to the Holy Spirit and to us to impose on the Gentiles no burden other than what is indispensable."* (Acts, 15:28) The Church does not want to cut off access to the Gospel by observances the spiritual life can do without.

But if we saw only that much in her eagerness for adaptation, we would be incapable of understanding her conduct; over and above that, her eagerness is inspired by a deeper principle, a requirement set up by the very catholicity of the Church. In fact, as we have seen, besides the artificial or passing differences which exist among human groupings as well as among individuals, there are fundamental differences which stem from a diversity of spiritual experience, and are expressed in thought, in art, in the organization of life. These are not arbitrary; they are the work of the Creator Himself Who has willed them to permit men to enrich themselves and give one another mutual help in the advance toward God. Now, it is in and by the Church that the Divine Plan is resumed after sin. Accordingly, the Church assumes all these differences by adapting herself to civilizations as well as to individuals, to render them fruitful and sanctify them all and lead them to their end.

True, there is no civilization (any more than there is any individual) to which the Christian life comes naturally. All have to be converted. The Gospel can never be received without renunciation, but Christian renunciation leads to life, not death. The Church is opposed only to the deviations, the corruptions, which disfigure the divine gift. Outside of her, the religious movement is always incomplete and more or less perverted. She wants to straighten it out in order to complete it. That involves some delicate work which can only be accomplished with sharp insight. The Church is thus at times obliged to call for prudence; the dispute concerning the Chinese and Malabaric rites is an example of that. Nevertheless, it is a necessary work. Pius XI insisted in a special way that wherever it take root, Christianity stand forth as truly native, and not as a foreign importation. This line of conduct is inspired by something quite other than political wisdom or a desire not to impose more than God demands. It fulfills one of the essential functions of the Church—that of returning to God all that is human.

And so, by another path, we arrive at a truth we have already noted in a previous conference—*Catholicism* is not just a religion, *it is religion.* Within its framework the religious impetus placed by God in each human being must find its term. This impetus is of identical substance in everyone, since it comes from the same God and returns to the same God, but it finds expression in natures which keep their originality. The Church orientates in the same direction the authentic spiritual resources she finds in each man. Only thus, consequently, can she bring to light all the riches she bears within herself.

When civilizations like those of India and China, for example, have been profoundly penetrated by the Church, then there will appear new and authentically Catholic forms of religious life; that is, forms truly inspired by the Church, expressing the same Faith in the same unity, but nonetheless different from those we know. This will then permit Christian values we now grasp poorly to be put in relief, and that will redound to the benefit of Christianity as a whole. For as we have seen, the Church does not limit herself to saving and developing each one in his own self. She sets up among everybody a current of communion, so much so that the treasures of each one profit all. Catholicity does not consist merely in the ability and the will to reach all men and all peoples, but in the ability and the will to assemble all into one, not in order to impose uniformity on them, but retaining instead their differences. Outside of her, these differences constantly lead to exasperating incomprehension and hostility. In her, they harmonize and complement one another.

A contemporary writer, J. Schlumberger, has written: "Christianity will eventually have to recognize that it cannot make a dent in certain great religions. . . . Everywhere on the surface of the globe the distribution of zones of influence is an accomplished fact, and sides have been taken. To leave behind one system of beliefs to adopt another is to change civilizations more than to change religions. Christianity will eventually have to accept the fact that it is linked to a culture and a way of thinking that are not universal." (*Sur les frontières religieuses*). There precisely is something the Church could not accept without ceasing to be herself. That would be to admit that she is made for only a portion of the universe and consequently, that mankind is bound to remain eternally divided or else be united outside of her. Both hypotheses she rejects under penalty of no longer being the Catholic Church. But, if she is able to make claims of that sort, it is because it is not necessary to "change civilizations" to enter her fold. Everyone need renounce only what is without value or is corrupt in himself. As for the remainder, the Church not only tolerates it—she positively wants it maintained. Opposed as she is, because she is Catholic, to all manner of divisions and to exclusiveness, she is opposed for the same reason to spiritual uniformity.

However, her children must not call down upon the Church misunderstandings of her attitude. *Catholicity must live in every Christian*. A real Catholic is not merely a person belonging to the Catholic Church. To be worthy of the name of Catholic is, first of all, to accept the differences of other people, to understand them, love them as such. It is to repudiate the sectarian spirit which gives an absolute and universal value to particularities. In order to discern in another what may be insignificant or else a deviation, the true Catholic consults the Church and not his personal preferences. He dreads nothing so much as cutting off access to the Church to someone, or rendering it more difficult for him, by having led him to believe, by his own manner of speaking or acting, that that person had to renounce things he is legitimately attached to. What is more, the true Catholic seeks, when the occasion presents itself, to enrich himself by means of the differences in other people; he does not believe he already possesses everything himself; he does not shut himself into himself. He does not concern himself with copying everything good that is done and thought elsewhere, but sees what portion of it he can assimilate. We must abide in this current of vital interchanges which passes through the whole Church, tap it as much as possible, and want it to be extended to the very limits of mankind.

To see in the Church merely a fine exterior organization is as we have said, to understand nothing at all about her. But it is just as radical and nefarious a misinterpretation to see in her just a sect, something partial which resigns itself to its limits and shuts itself up within those limits, when in fact she wants to penetrate everything in order to unite and vivify everything by means of fruitful interchanges.

6

The Sanctity of the Church

One of the titles we give the Church in our Creed is that of Holy: *Credo in Spiritum Sanctum . . . sanctam Ecclesiam catholicam.* And this characteristic of sanctity she possesses is one of the reasons behind the love and admiration we have for her.

The presence of sin in the Church

The Church is holy, we say. But, not only does she live in the midst of a sinful world, a world where sin abounds. We are even forced, are we not, to say that she herself is afflicted and even gangrenous with sin? She has sinful members who really are part of her Body, whom she claims as hers. If we were to adopt the idea of an invisible Church made up only of the just, the members of which would be known to God alone, Who alone reads the secret of hearts, we would have a ready answer. "Unworthy Christians," we would say, "are not really part of the Church; they seem to belong, but in

75

reality they are strangers to her." The desire to keep the Church away from all contact with evil, and the suffering experienced at the thought that there can be men who claim to be hers while at the same time they drag out their lives in sin, these no doubt count for something, sometimes for much, in this dream of an invisible Church. But the Catholic Church herself, which affirms her own prerogative of holiness, forbids us this bit of escapism. Such a concept, we have seen, contradicts God's Plan, the Will of Christ which is to communicate His life by means of the Sacraments through the intermediary of a visibly constituted organism. The motherly Church does not reject sinners from her bosom as long as they do not withdraw themselves. This is true to the extent that a great many of the miseries found among non-Christians are found also in the Church. Not only are there misunderstandings, old-wiveries, prejudices, all, doubtless, marks of human weakness, but which remain reconcilable with real virtue; there are also sins and vices properly so called. These reign not only among the least members of the Church—they sometimes invade the ranks of the Hierarchy. If, for quite a while now, we have had the joy of seeing in the Chair of Peter Popes worthy, because of their virtues, of being models for those entrusted to them, we know that this was not always so. It would serve no purpose to try to cover up the failings of all kinds which members and leaders of the Church have displayed. History discovers and describes them. Moreover, it is not only because such an attempt would be in vain that we must refuse to deny them. The Christian everywhere respects the truth— that is a virtue which the Church teaches him, just as Jesus Christ used to inculcate it in His disciples: *Sit sermo vester, est, est; non, non.* We must not here resort to embarrassed explanations. We need only recognize the facts loyally and humbly. We could draw a sad picture, a picture to crush the heart of a true son of the Church, the truth of which, however, he could not deny.

We are sometimes scandalized to see this picture traced by Christian hands. I believe that in this, everything depends on the intention, on the spirit in which it is done. We will not speak of the ironic amusement which would be had in raking up this muck—such a sentiment would be unworthy not only of a Christian, but even of a human being. (When it happens that a Christian is obliged to delve into the evil which exists outside the Church, even in circles and organizations which fight against her, he must do so only with sadness, with sorrow. A note of triumph in pointing out moral weaknesses, even of an implacable enemy, always wounds a heart truly human, *a fortiori* a Christian heart). Neither must we add a note of bitterness, of resentment, a spirit of disparagement which indicates that the filial spirit has disappeared. It is necessary to note what is there because it is there, not with a sort of indifference of sentiment which might be taken for scientific impartiality—loyally admitting what is and remaining indifferent to it are two things which have nothing in common. Though he suffers profoundly because of it, the Christian can turn a clear eye upon the weaknesses and blemishes which History reveals.

It is thus that, in his own way, he bears testimony to the worth of the Faith he has received and to the Church whence he obtained it. His courageous loyalty demonstrates to everybody the confidence he has in his

Church: people see that his Faith is not lessened by such a spectacle because he is able to see further and deeper. Let us never allow those on the outside to suppose that if we believe, it is because we have turned our eyes away from incontestable facts. Our confidence in the Church must not rest on ignorance of reality. No doubt there is —and we must never forget this—an age for every kind of knowledge. To neglect this psychological fact would be not to worship the truth but to exhibit a temerarious disdain of the conditions in which the truth must be received into a mind in order to penetrate it without travesty. But the trained adult Christian, both as a man and as a Christian, must be able to face squarely, objectively, the history of the Church as well as her present state. And it is to be desired that every Christian become someday an adult Christian.

You can see that I in no way wish to gloss over the existence of sinners in the Church, the presence of sin in the Body of the Church. Once again, I believe that the fact that there is a Christian who can say: "I have faced squarely all the miserable facts of our history; I know everything serious you can bring out on that score, and yet that does not prevent me from saying with full consciousness and full reflection, every time I say my Creed: *Credo sanctam Ecclesiam*"; I believe that that is a fact calculated to cause the unbeliever or the believer whose Faith might waver at the sight of so much weakness, to reflect. He will be led to ask himself if after all he might not be mistaken as to the importance he attaches to what he sees, since someone else who also sees it finds in his Faith itself the explanation for what baffles or scandalizes him. Just what is it, therefore, that prevents the believer from being disconcerted?

The Presence of Sanctity within the Church

Its reality: In order to understand this let us start by establishing something else—something moreover, that the unbeliever himself can discover but from which he will doubtless not draw the same light. If there is sin in the Church, if there are sinful members, there is also holiness, and we must look on that with the same loyalty as upon the evil. (Holiness, however, is not always so easy to see, even when it abounds, because it is less flamboyant, and because it finds us less willing to correspond to it). It sometimes happens that even the good Christian does not give it the place it deserves, does not see it in all its splendor. It is perhaps because he considers it altogether natural to find it in the Church that he looks upon it as self-evident—something upon which it is therefore unnecessary to dwell.

Still, it is important to bring ourselves to esteem it at its true value, to admire it as it deserves. It is preferable not to consider it only on the outside and from afar, but to make an effort to understand it enough to catch a glimpse of the degree to which it has raised man.

First of all, much could be said at this point on the moral value the Church has helped to give even to those who do not belong to her. She has revealed to the world a new ideal of life, and this not only by means of her doctrinal teachings, but because her children have made this ideal known, have put it in the limelight, have created a taste for it by living it before the world. A simple exposition, a mere exhortation, would not have been sufficient.

In some of the most beautiful pages of "The Two Sources," Bergson has shown how new moral values

are propagated: by the appeal of the hero who lives
them. His practice *is* his appeal; the spectacle he gives
creates in those who do not shut themselves off from it,
a nostalgia for what is better, while revealing to them
a quality of life they would otherwise never have suspected. No one contests the fact that, under the influence of the Church, the examples given by those who
have lived by her have led mankind to take a decisive
step forward in the appreciation of moral values. Thus it
is that this same Church in which we could see so many
sinful members, so many scandals, reveals herself at the
same time as the great moral teacher of mankind. And
we do not have the right to say: she used to be that way
in the days of her fervor, but she is not like that nowadays. For who could pretend, if he knew the facts a
little, that the course of her history is one of progressive
decadence? She has had, if we consider her externally,
her ups and downs, her periods of decadence and of
reform. There is consequently no reason for localizing
her influence for good in a far-distant past. Without her,
the moral values currently recognized even among many
of those who do not formally belong to her, would not
be what they are. This is so true that it is often in the
name of the demands she herself has given rise to, that
people reproach the Church for the weaknesses evident
in her. That is a fact which must hold our attention; it
shows that we have before us a unique case. But we must
force ourselves to see directly and for its own sake, this
flowering of sanctity within the Church. It is impossible
to describe it, even quite summarily; impossible to cat-
alogue it even rather incompletely. It will be of more
value to underline a few of the traits which characterize
it.

A few of these traits: First of all, we must not fail to recognize its actual extent. We have said that in the Church, besides the sinners there are unfortunately many who are mediocre. But in like manner, alongside the heights of sanctity, there is a mass of faithful whose importance we cannot minimize, to whom the Church has given a serious and solid moral life, a whole ensemble of opinions and virtues, and that is in itself far from negligible. As to the heights of sanctity, these are not rare exceptions in the history of the Church, but form a continuous chain. Even in the saddest periods of her history, the Church has seen sanctity flourish. In this matter, the canonized saints are only a small part. Sanctity is truly catholic; it appears in all the civilizations which Christ has touched, in every degree of culture, in all conditions and states of life, among the members of the Hierarchy as well as among the humblest of the faithful. It finds expression in extremely varied characters. If Christians have the painful duty of recognizing that the Chair of Saint Peter was at times occupied by unworthy men, yet, thank God, there has been no lack of saints—that list is long and glorious. The Church has everywhere and at all times spread abroad sanctity, and that applies not only to ancient history—the immediate past of the Church in no way gives the impression that her sanctifying power is on the decline.

This Catholic holiness is above all an interior affair. Still it is not a force which aims only at the interior transformation of the individual, as if it had not to concern itself with the transformation of the world, with the Christianization of human institutions, even national and international. She has worked on that in every century, and in many ways. That is only one aspect of the matter, but it is not negligible. True, we have not today arrived at an acceptable state of affairs! And I do not even pretend that all fervent Christians have always been conscious of the duty incumbent upon them of acting on the world. For a goodly number of them, we might even speak of a certain "social quietism," that is to say, a persuasion at least in practice, that it is possible to sanctify oneself without in any way having to combat the injustice reigning all around. Whatever may be said of this illusion, which is an error of spirituality since it prevents the recognition of the full extent of the law of Charity, it is clear that the influence of the Church has not been limited to the creating of little islands of personal holiness without any action on the world.

Many institutions unacceptable to human dignity have disappeared or have been transformed under the influence of Christian ideas lived and propagated by real Christians. And the very intensity of the feeling with which we today consider what is unacceptable in the present state of the world, bears witness that in this domain, too, the Church's activity has not been inefficacious. The socialisms most hostile to the Church could not have arisen in a society untouched by Christianty, (and that is recognized by many socialists). I do not believe that the revolt of a Karl Marx against the spectacle he had before his eyes, can be explained without taking into account the fact that, willy-nilly, he had been subject to Christian influences. The holiness produced by the Church has therefore spread its rays in the world.

A correct notion of it. Is it enough, however, to contrast the existence of Christian holiness and the admission of sin in the Church? No. For the Christian, what is essential is the matter of their relationship, their respective places in the bosom of this society which is the Church, and not their quantitative proportions, as it were. It is from this (relationship) that he obtains light. In fact, what people will be tempted to bring up to him as an objection is the fact that this society contains a mixture of good and evil, and the balance sheet drawn up for it will seem more positive or more negative according as one's attention is drawn more forcibly to one of the two aspects. The Christian rejects such a method of procedure. If he accepted it, it could lead him to a paradoxical consequence: as it happens, since evil has not always existed in the same degree in the Church, the conclusion would be that the Church should be called more or less holy depending on the epoch in which we consider her. But in the Creed we say: "*sanctam Ecclesiam*" in an absolute sense. The Church is always holy, always just as holy in herself, always absolutely holy we can even say, no matter what may be her present status in individuals. That is because Faith teaches us not to see her as the product of the men who make her up. That, however, is the implied premise we start from when, to evaluate her degree of holiness, we make up a balance sheet of the virtues and vices of Catholics at any given time.

The Church is the mysterious organism by which Divine Charity is implanted in humanity to uplift and transform it. She is, as we have said, Redemption on the march, Redemption in action. Thus, we must expect to find in her, as two elements, the purifying and sanctifying Divine Force, and the human mass to which this force is applied in order to transform it. If we separate these two elements there is no more Church! On one

side there is now only an unemployed force with no
action on the world, and on the other a mass given over
to sin, where no leaven of radical transformation is at
work. If there is really a Church, it is because the
Divine Force attains sinners, thanks to the intervention
of sensible, visible instruments, thanks to a Hierarchy
which teaches and administers the Sacraments.

You see, however, that these two elements are not in
the same order, are not on the same plane. It is impossible to weigh them to see which has the edge on the
other. Christian holiness already achieved represents that
part of the human mass which has let itself be transformed by active acquiescence. The sinful members, or
what remains of sin in those who have nevertheless begun to let themselves be taken over by grace, are like the
residue—the non-transformed part, the evil which has
resisted, which still resists. But the holiness realized in
the members of the Church is not itself the holiness of
the Church—it is only the effect and the manifestation
thereof. It flows from the essential holiness we speak
about primarily when we say: *credo sanctam Ecclesiam*.
Besides, let us add that this essential holiness in turn is
the holiness of the Church only because it is at work in
mankind, and because its action is efficacious insofar as
human liberty lets it be. Moreover, we know that it will
never fail to have some real effect.

Its action on the world. If the souls with whom the
Church comes in contact put up no resistance to her, the
world would be transformed in the exact measure in
which the preaching of the Gospel would reach it, and
the fertility of the Church would never be exhausted,
because the Church never ceases receiving the power to
sanctify every human being, and leading each one even

to the highest perfection. Her holiness is infinite, that is to say, it is never exhausted by communicating itself, because the holiness she communicates is the one she has received from Christ Who is her Head, and from the Holy Spirit Who is her Soul.

But there are men who refuse the Church, who reject her light because their works are evil and because they prefer darkness to the light, as St. John says, (which does not mean, we may recall, that all those who have refused external adherence to the Church have rejected the light. It is well-nigh impossible, in many cases, to know if the Church has been authentically presented to them according to her "real appearance"). That is why, despite the Church, there is evil in the world.

Many men who allow themselves to be touched by her influence, who accept her Faith and are incorporated into her by Baptism, do not for all that let the grace of the Sacraments blossom out in them. Very soon they put up a resistance—being more or less conscious of their evil wills, and that is why there are in the Church so many who are lukewarm, so many who are mediocre. Many baptized people also, people who hold to her Faith and do not want to be separated from it, nevertheless lead a life contrary to the logic of this Faith, a life opposed to that which the grace of their Baptism seeks to arouse in them. They let themselves descend to evildoing at the beck and call of circumstances and of their own temptations, and that is why there are so many sinners in the Church. They resist the action of the Church in them. That does not prevent the Church from being a power for holiness, a power of infinite holiness capable of wholly regenerating them, even of wiping out all the evil in their lives. Certain among these sinners may occupy a place in her Hierarchy, and then there is a painful contrast between the sanctity their functions demand and what they are themselves. But that does not prevent them, when they agree to act as ministers of the Church, from being instruments, however unworthy, of a sanctifying action. They are hurting themselves, not those to whom they communicate the holy things.

All those—the lukewarm, the mediocre, the sinners—the Church does not reject. She never makes the first move toward a break. Not that she needs them; rather, they need her, and can still benefit by her kindnesses. For as long as they are in this life, their state is not hopeless—they are not definitely established in evil. The link she maintains with them by means of the Faith they preserve is a way of acting upon them. She recalls to them the exigencies of this Faith, she warns them of the fate which awaits the sinner. Because they still believe, her word can reach them, though it does not act infallibly, for they remain free. Be that as it may, their sin does not overflow onto her, does not contaminate her. The resistance put up by her own members to her sanctifying activity does not take away from the fact that she possesses always in her Faith and her Sacraments, the doctrine of holiness and the source of holiness, for her formulas of Faith and her sacramental rites are something visible, striking.

The Church therefore does not shun contact with the sinner, as though he would besmirch her. On the contrary, she is on the lookout for him because she is holy enough to purify him from his sin. She goes to meet the sinner who lives far from her. She accepts the sinner who continues to live in her without breaking the bond of Faith, while awaiting her chance to transform him. If she goes in search of the lost sheep, she does not repulse the recalcitrant sheep but struggles to bring it back to liberating obedience. That is how the Church views the sinner; that is how we must look upon him. His presence does not sully her, but serves as a proof of her Charity. It does not show up her weakness or her laxity but the freedom of man who can oppose grace. It is necessary to understand correctly the position of the sinner in the Church. Sometimes we dream of a Church which, in order to maintain her purity and holiness, would expel the unworthy from her bosom, and declare that she has nothing in common with them. In this dream there is to begin with a good bit of Pharisaism.

We should first of all believe that our own mediocrity undoubtedly does not honor the Church very much, that it is hardly likely to cause her holiness to shine forth. We would readily draw the line of exclusion just below ourselves, but should we not perhaps place it a bit above us, so that the honor of the Church might be above reproach, if this honor consisted in her not counting either sinners or the mediocre among her members? And does not the mediocre person who thus spurns the sinner take a chance by that very fact, of descending below him? If he himself worked toward holiness, if at the same time he acquired a greater horror of sin, he would doubtless, following the pattern of the Church, become more indulgent . . .

But this is a question of lack of recognition of the nature and functions of the Church. She is not constituted merely to give a show of holiness to the world, to contrast her integrity with the corruption of men. She is made to save the world. She is made to save this mass.

If she receives as a heritage the holiness of the Father, the Son and the Holy Spirit, it is not in order to set it in defiant opposition to the world, but in order to communicate it to the world. And so she does not flee to the desert nor does she shut herself up in cloisters. She descends into this mass in order to penetrate it, in order to act upon it.

Sometimes she runs up against complete refusal. At other times she is only imperfectly understood, imperfectly accepted, or else people half-detach themselves from her—they preserve the Faith she has handed down, without living it. The Church suffers from all these different kinds of refusal. She suffers particularly from the attitude of the children Baptism has given her who refuse the life she offers them. But for all that she does not disown them because she is a loving mother who wants, despite everything, to save them. Would she be putting herself in a position to act more effectively on them by cutting off all links with them, by turning them out? In practice, pastors are faced with cases of conscience in knowing how to dole out indulgence and salutary warnings.

But so long as her children hold on to her by Faith, so long as they recognize the principle of her authority, the Church will not tell them: You no longer belong. That would be a betrayal, on her part, of her mission; that would be veiling or minimizing the exigencies of Christian life in order to hold on or draw men to herself. But she has always refused to do that. To cite but one example, she refused to compromise on the indissolubility of marriage, even to hold on to a Henry VIII of England, although his defection would draw all of England into schism. For what she wants is to sanctify her sinful members; but, by hiding their duty from them, by compromising the demands of the moral law or of Christian perfection, she would be giving up trying to lead them back to goodness.

Now we understand this much, that however miserable many of her members may be, she ever remains the Holy Church. By her Faith and by her Sacraments, by her organization destined to serve these, she ever remains the implantation in the world of the sanctifying power of God, the visible organism of holiness. She is the Spouse, spotless and immaculate, whom Christ has washed with His Blood, to whom He has confided this redeeming Blood. Faith alone can see her in this way. But to repeat once more, it is from the viewpoint of Faith and Faith alone that we really understand what the Church is. The believer who explains to the unbeliever what his Faith in the Church is, can at least make him understand why the facts he beholds here and there are not of such a nature as to trouble him, without there being any need, however, for him to shut his eyes. Besides, the day will come when the holiness of the Church will shine forth in all her members. That will not come about, however, before the end of time. As long as she lives in the midst of this world, the Church will pull along her train of misery.

But a time is coming for each of her members when a definite choice will have to be made. Those who will have resisted to the end her sanctifying action will not be part of the Church of heaven. Those who will have consented to it only imperfectly will have to be purified before entering into her. The Church of Eternity will be wholly pure and immaculate in her members. In the Church of Time, there will be to the end a mixture of good and evil, though in differing proportions, but the sanctifying power will ever be present and always acting.

That is why the Church, in her great crises, reforms herself. That is why there are always in her fold Christians who suffer because of the state she is in, because of the insufficient glow coming from the hearthplace of holiness she possesses. These however do not conclude therefrom to the non-existence or insufficiency of this hearth; they blame it on the bad will of men, not, however, merely to curse it, but to transform it. Few pages could be found that are harder on the abuses and failings of the Church than those written by a St. Peter Damian or a St. Bernard. But it is from the Church herself that these great reformers of the Church have caused to spring forth the flame that was to renew her. Whether it be Gregory VII, or the flowering of the Mendicant Orders with St. Dominic and St. Francis of Assisi, or those who fashioned what we call the Counter-Reformation or the Christian renewal of the 17th century, it is always essentially the same manner of acting—it is a matter of finding in the Church the remedy for the illnesses of the Church, because the remedy for the sin which afflicts her lies only in the holiness she possesses.

That is a great lesson, to be remembered at all times. We can, we must suffer because of the mediocrity and the sins of her members, because of the fact that her action fails to take an efficacious grasp on the world, because of the lack of consciousness of so many Christians to the moral problems posed by the state of society, because of the lack of interest they show in the evils of the age, and the little they do to remedy them, because of their frequent inertia before injustice, their timidity and at times their laxity in the face of this triumphant injustice. But, even when we put things at their worst, by supposing the greatest scandals (history can attest to some of this type), it would be foolish, for all that, for us to draw away from the Church. That would be to abandon the source of holiness, the only source whence that can come, under the pretext that its effects are not sufficiently felt. If holiness is really the only efficacious force capable of combatting sin and with it, the woes and injustices that are its consequences, how would our work be effective if we cut ourselves off from the source of holiness?

We must on the contrary begin by drawing from that source, we must draw from it all the more the tougher the battle appears to be. We have to tell ourselves that in order to put our shoulders to the task of transforming the world, we must start by leaving ourselves open to the transforming force which is holiness. Otherwise we expose ourselves to the worst of disappointments—for ourselves as well as for others. When a serious number of Christians has come to a lively awareness that the Christian milieu is not what it should be, that its hold on the world that surrounds it is not sufficiently strong, when they are decided to make their lives a means whereby the holiness of the Church can shine forth, then we can foresee magnificent rebirths. But to seek to remedy the evils of the Church and the world by an activity which is pursued outside the Church, or which fails to draw upon the source of holiness, is wasted effort.

You see that when we speak of sin in the Church or of holiness within the Church, we are not speaking of two things that oppose and counterbalance one another in the same order. Sin is only too naturally explained by this force of sin which St. Paul so vividly describes for us in the Epistle to the Romans, a force to which mankind abandons itself. The holiness of the members of the Church is the sign, the revelation of the holiness of the Church, which itself comes from the Holiness of the Father, the Son and the Holy Spirit. This holiness of the members consists in whatever part of the holiness of the Church they consent to let pass into them; it is that part of themselves that they have opened to her sanctifying power. Mankind remains free. Likewise, darkness can prevent the light from shining everywhere, but the light does not exist any the less for all that, and with an infinite shining power. The source of holiness is not any less inexhaustible at all times. Despite all the deficiencies of her members, the Church is holy and sanctifying; and the more we generously let ourselves be transformed, the more too we believe in her divine reality, the more we will be persuaded that there is no need of searching elsewhere to transform the world.

7

The Role of the Hierarchy
in the Church

The Hierarchy goes back to Christ

Christ is the Head of the Church which is His Body. But, since His Ascension, He is invisible, inaccessible to our senses. He makes the Church live by His Spirit, but we do not perceive Him in the same way the Apostles saw Him guiding their little band. The Spirit He sends His Church, Who is her soul and life-giving center, is Himself also invisible. Nevertheless, the Church is not a society whose members are left alone to themselves under the sole direction of the invisible Christ. All do not have the same role in it, all are not on the same level; just as there is among them a hierarchy of holiness— which is known to God—there is also a visible Hierarchy, social and external.

This Hierarchy has always existed

The Church has never been, even for a short time, as some have imagined, a society in which religious enthusiasm, interior inspiration, was the only law, so that the determination of authority with its train of laws and regulations would have appeared only when the original fire had subsided, the first impetus died down. There did exist in the primitive Church a series of exterior spiritual manifestations, some of which are of a character quite disconcerting to us. St. Paul, who calls them "charisms," bears witness to their abundance, an abundance at times intemperate since he sees himself obliged to regulate their expression (First Epistle to the Corinthians). Note moreover that he places Charity above all the charisms. The habitual presence of these charisms in the first Christian communities is explained by providential circumstances and at the same time, they bear the mark of the environment in which they appear. Their disappearance takes nothing essential away from the Church. They are of value as helps, or as manifestations of the intensity of spiritual life, that is to say, in short, as manifestations of the intensity of Charity. But Charity, on the other hand, has value of itself. It is not necessarily diminished by their disappearance, for it can express itself in other ways.

Before or after the disappearance of the charisms, there has always existed in the Church a visible Hierarchy not bound up with these charisms. Christ Himself is at its source by means of the functions He confided to the Apostolic College, with Peter at its head. What is essential to this Hierarchy has therefore existed since the beginning, although its forms and expression have varied very much in adapting themselves to the conditions in which the life of the Church was lived, to the very exigencies of her growth and to the complexity caused by her development. It is an important task to demonstrate the divine foundation of the ecclesiastical Hierarchy, and its continuity in its essential organisms from the time of the Apostles, in line with the expression of the Creed: *et apostolicam Ecclesiam.* It is not the task I will take on here, at least directly. Our purpose is not to write history—though this is very necessary for apologetics and very useful for a wider knowledge—but rather to try to penetrate our Faith.

The first thing for a Christian to do in the presence of the fact that there is a Hierarchy whose subject he is, is to understand its meaning, to grasp its religious role. It is thus that he will see what his conduct towards it must be. The Hierarchy must not be accepted simply as a fact, and especially must it not be endured as a fate involving a painful obligation to submit which is not really ratified deep down inside. Doubtless, it will always be more or less painful for us to obey. But if we have seen how the leadership of the Hierarchy is necessary for our religious life, then we will love the sacrifice demanded of us. It will remain painful for the carnal man, but it will be a joy for the spiritual man. How then are we to understand the Catholic Hierarchy?

The Meaning of the Hierarchy

There is, then, authority in the Church. This, we might think, is quite natural and contains no mystery. Only Utopians can believe that a group of any sort can live without authority, and the fatal disintegration of all societies of any complexity at all which try to exempt themselves from this law, removes this illusion. A religious society therefore must have, it is clear, a religious authority to insure order and common direction in it; an authority like all others except that it is exercised on the religious instead of the civil plane. It seems to me that that is the principle a liberal Protestantism might place as the basis of authority in the Church when it does recognize one. In fact, if the Church is the grouping together of Christians who assemble to strengthen one another mutually in the spiritual life, we can scarcely see how there could be any other principle.

We could simply add that alongside the function of governing, other equally indispensable religious functions would have to appear. As a matter of fact, if there is Worship at all complex in a somewhat numerous group, then it is necessary that someone be charged with it and consecrate himself to it, since the majority of the faithful are taken up with their particular occupations. From this there arises some sort of priesthood of service in Worship, no matter what name we may give to it. Moreover, not all the faithful have the time or the chance to give themselves over to religious studies advanced enough to permit them to inventory for themselves the contents of revelation (represented, for the Protestants, by the Bible alone); to know how to find therein the answer to new questions, or at least the answer to the old questions asked in a new way. Certain persons will therefore have to consecrate themselves to this work and they will then make the others benefit by their knowledge—in this sense, they will teach them. It seems, therefore, that authority and the functions of worship and teaching are necessary consequences of the existence of a religious society. If God has willed this religious society, He has also willed its conditions. It can then be said that this authority and these other functions which have in this way been set up within the society have a divine value. That much can be said of civil society, the State, whose existence is willed by God as necessary for the truly human existence of man, indispensable to humanity which must pursue on earth the progress willed for it by God.

But this is borne out in another sense; for if a religious society be willed by Christ, to prolong the action which He began during the course of His earthly life, it must be said as a consequence that authority and the other religious functions of this society are equally willed by Christ.

What objection can we have against these considerations? Simply that they are *inadequate*. They have value, on the basis of experience and common thought, against those who might envision a religious society wherein there would be no differentiation. But they do not permit us to penetrate the meaning of the Catholic Hierarchy. They do not reveal to us its relationship to Christ. That is because in this matter as elsewhere, if one wishes really to understand a reality which is "ecclesiastical" in the full sense of that word, that is to say, a reality belonging to and characteristic of, the Church, then one has to begin by having a precise, exact idea of the Church. We must not consider her merely as a society which, having a religious purpose, must meet on the religious plane the requirements common to every society. *We must see her relationship to Christ*, a relationship which constitutes her in her original and unique reality.

Christ, we have already said, did not found the
Church just once upon a time, as a man founds a human society which owes him its existence in the past but
thereafter lives and develops without him. Jesus Christ
remains the Head of the Church. He remains the Chief
who instructs her, sanctifies her, directs her. He dwells
with her "until the consummation of the world." It is
true, in one sense, to say that He does this by means of
His Spirit. But He also does it by means of the Hierarchy which He established. Nor are these two separate
means coming alternately into play. They are two means
bound together, inseparable, representing as it were,
the visible and invisible aspects of the action of Christ
on His Church. That is why, as Fr. Congar says in his
"Esquisses du Mystere de l'Eglise," p. 35: "It is not
only sensible inanimate means, thing-sacraments, that
Christ uses to perfect His Mystical Body, but it is also,
and by the same logic, sensible animate means, person-
sacraments. The Church is not only sacramental, she is
apostolic and hierarchic." That is very exact—provided
of course that it be properly understood. When the
members of the Catholic Hierarchy act in the exercise
of the power confided to them by Christ, or, if you will,
when they act under certain conditions which are not
arbitrary but fixed by the Will of Christ Himself, it is
the action of Christ which reaches us through them. It
is His teaching action, His sanctifying action, His commands.

God has not promised the men designated for such
functions that He would take away their human weaknesses. What is more, even when they act rightly, their
actions are not for all that always the vehicles of Christ's
action. They have their personal opinions, their prefer-

ences, just as every man may have, and these, even when they are legitimate, are not necessarily Christ's ideas. We do not deify men even when they are irreproachable and virtuous. But what we are saying is that under certain given conditions, their acts, their teaching, their orders are the vehicles of Christ's action, of His teaching, of His Will. They are not merely men who command other men because a religious society, as every other society, needs a specialized authoritative function. They bring down to us Christ's own action; through them, this action reaches us. And that is what constitutes the proper characteristic of their authority. It is this particular link with Christ which gives the Catholic Hierarchy its meaning. Even the action of Christ which He exercises through His Spirit is bound up with the intervention of these men.

Thus we are always coming back to the bond between the visible and the invisible in the Church, that is to say, in the action which Christ is exercising today in the midst of our humanity. The first of these two elements has no value and no meaning by itself, but only by means of the invisible element which it contains, which it secures, of which it is the means of realization. That is true of this matter, though in a different way, as it is of the water used in Baptism or of the sensible species in the Eucharist. (Baptismal water, however, does not bear the same relationship to grace as the eucharistic species bear to the Body of Christ, but in the one case as in the other, it is a matter of "signs," of "sacraments"). By the same token, the invisible element is normally bound up with the visible.

It is in this sense that we can speak of "person-sacraments"—not that all the actions of these persons are so many means whereby Christ leads His Church, but that this leadership is bound up with certain actions of these persons, actions which imply awareness, will, liberty. There is the reason why the existence of the Hierarchy is not looked upon by the true Christian as a burden, a heavy drag on his religious life, but on the contrary as a help and a grace; for by means of it, he comes in contact with Christ and puts himself under His vivifying and liberating influence. The Hierarchy is not an interme-diary that might prove to be an obstacle between Christ and himself; it is the means by which he is bound to Christ. Assuredly, it is only Faith which makes him be-hold Christ's action in the action of the Hierarchy. Just as in a Sacrament, the visible element veils over the in-visible grace while at the same time it is its sign, it can also be said that the existence of the visible Hierarchy is like a veil which hides from us the action of Christ. But we cannot say that it takes us far away or separates us from Him. And if we are asked why this veil, we must simply answer: *Because we are in a period of Faith*, of trial; we are in the earthly stage. We must recognize Christ when He veils Himself in order one day to merit seeing Him face to face and experiencing His action di-rectly, in all clarity.

Let us note also that the one who refuses the Hier-archy because he wants direct communication with God, with Christ, hoping to find it in interior experi-ence, that man is in the path of illusion. Interior experi-ence is always a bit confusing—how to discern with accuracy the voice of God, that of Christ, from our own voice, the voice of our caprices or of our human dreams? Catholicism does not deny at all that there is interior inspiration; however, when it has been nourished, it has still to be controlled, disciplined, corrected if need be. We have to make a distinction between what really comes from God, what we can have confidence in, and what comes from ourselves. But it is precisely the Hierarchy which, with its teachings, and as a last resort, its decisions, permits us to make this distinction. It therefore permits us to make use of interior inspiration; far from suppressing it, it uncovers it.

There again, it is important to understand clearly how a Catholic views the Hierarchy if we wish to understand the nature of the sentiments which attach him to it. This attachment is not found in the need for human support; it does not proceed from the fear of personal initiative (we will discuss this more at length); it is not the doing of a childish or a slavish soul. It has its source in *the will to submit oneself to Christ*, to remain subject to His illuminating and sanctifying action, to know what He expects from us, what is His Will for us. Submission to the Hierarchy, the acceptance of its decisions, may be difficult because it is one of the means whereby Christ enters into our life, and this always wounds our egoism, always mortifies in us what St. Paul calls the "carnal man." But it is a joy for the spiritual man whom it continues to liberate, a joy for whatever in us belongs to God or wants to belong to God.

That is the explanation also for the respect which the Christian has for all the members of the Hierarchy. He knows very well, as we have said, that they are not in every phase of their activity the representatives of Christ, and he retains his freedom with regard to the opinions and the preferences which they might manifest even in religious matters, as private persons. But he everywhere and always respects them because of this action of Christ of which they are the instruments. Even outside of the sacrifice, we never treat a chalice as an ordinary object. It is an analogous sentiment which inspires the attitude of the faithful not only towards the decisions or the teachings of the Hierarchy, but towards the persons who have, in some degree, the mission of formulating and transmitting them.

Respect is never expressed by anything resembling flattery. That is even out of place with regard to human authority, *a fortiori* is it out of place with regard to those whom we venerate because of Christ Whom they represent. The depth of the respect we have for them loses nothing by maintaining a certain sobriety in its expression, and it is to corrupt it to fall into obsequiousness—this latter is not religious, whereas the respect the faithful have for the members of the Hierarchy is something of a religious nature. Naturally, this respect does not depend upon what they are themselves, and it must not be influenced by the human sentiments we may experience towards them.

The Catholic Hierarchy was instituted by Christ when He established the Apostles, the "Twelve," with Peter at their head. These transmitted their powers to their successors, who are the Bishops. One of these, the Bishop of Rome, is the successor of Peter. Always and in all places, in the exercise of their authority the members of the Hierarchy are the "ministers of Christ." Whatever be the manner in which they are designated (that has changed very much in the course of twenty centuries of history), they are not delegated by the religious community to exercise the functions necessary for its existence. They are the means, the channels, which Jesus Christ uses to act in His Church. In her, everything comes from God through Christ. It is not of themselves, in virtue of their own efforts, that the members of the Church sanctify themselves, participate in divine life, are introduced into the life of the Trinity. It is God, it is Christ, Who, by His grace (with their free co-operation) Who sanctifies, elevates, divinizes them. The Hierarchy, being the means by which grace is communicated to us, cannot be established except by Christ.

The Hierarchy exercises a triple function, and consequently is endowed with a threefold power: the power of teaching, which we also call the Magisterium; the power of Orders, which is concerned with the offering of Sacrifice and the administration of the Sacraments; the power of jurisdiction, which bears upon the internal government of the Church. Let us say a word about these three powers.

The Functions of the Hierarchy

Power of teaching. The role of the Magisterium is *to preserve intact the deposit of Faith*, to keep it from all corruption, to teach the faithful, to prevent them from going astray in their beliefs, to make them grow in the Faith. We can understand the importance and necessity of this function when we also understand the primal place of Faith in the Christian life; it is to insure its exercise that the Magisterium is endowed by the assistance of the Holy Spirit, with the privilege of infallibility. Doubtless, the Church taken as a whole, is infallible, in the sense that the Church as a whole will never accept a doctrine contrary to Faith. But that does not exclude the fact that we must distinguish in her the Teaching Church and the Church Taught. The Teaching Church is precisely the Hierarchy insofar as it has the function of teaching the faithful. This teaching refers only to questions bearing on the religious life, that is to say, on the truths of Faith, or truths accessible to reason the upholding of which is important for the preservation of the truths of Faith (for example, the existence of God, the immortality of the soul). It is evidently necessary to include among the truths of Faith those which refer to conduct.

The Bishops reunited in General Council ("oecumenical" council) are infallible, and their teachings do not need to be ratified by the assembly of the faithful in order to be infallible. The Pope speaking *ex cathedra*, that is to say, as the Teacher of the Universal Church with the formal intention of teaching a point of doctrine as forming part of the Faith, is infallible, and his teaching too, under these conditions, does not need to be submitted for the assent of the Bishops in order to be binding.

Alongside these methods of proceeding, which are relatively rare, and which pertain to what is called the extraordinary exercise of the Magisterium, there is its ordinary exercise, the one which is carried out by means of the teaching which the Hierarchy on all levels gives in the ordinary course of the life of the Church. A teaching which comes from the whole Hierarchy, that is, from the whole Church, through the ordinary Magisterium, cannot be false, for that would indicate that those who are charged with stimulating the Faith of the believers, had themselves fallen into error. But the existence of a power of teaching founded by Christ has for its very purpose the avoidance of just such straying away. But we must nevertheless realize that many doctrinal decisions, either because they emanate from just a few members of the Hierarchy, or if they come from the Pope, because he does not intend to impose them on the Universal Church, do not possess the note of infallibility. Often even, though their content is doctrinal, they are only of a disciplinary nature; for example, it might be forbidden to teach, to propagate such and such a doctrine. Without wishing to commit itself as to the core of such doctrines, the Hierarchy thinks that in certain determinate circumstances, given the state of the question and the condition of minds, they are dangerous to Faith. Such decisions are obviously not irrevocable, which does not of course mean that we are not to pay any attention to them. In all this, we must neither try to exempt ourselves from the authority of the Hierarchy, nor give to its decisions a bearing which itself it does not give them. It is a common pitfall among zealous but little-informed laymen (as also among those on the outside), this exaggeration of the properly doctrinal scope of that type of decision. Trained theologians are generally more reserved. Let us always remember that the function of the Magisterium is to bring down to us the teaching of Christ, the thought of Christ. It is in this way that we must see it in order to accept its decisions.

The Power of Orders. The second function of the Hierarchy is one of sanctification and is insured by the power of Orders. This power is essentially concerned with the administration of the Sacraments. Of course, it is not only the members of the Hierarchy, Bishops or priests, who can administer the Sacraments. All men can validly confer Baptism, and do so licitly in case of necessity; and it is the spouses who are reciprocally the ministers of the Sacrament of Matrimony. But to get right down to essentials, let us say that it is to the Hierarchy, insofar as it is endowed with the power of Orders, that Our Lord has given power over His Body in the Eucharist. This is so true that we can say that the power of Orders is the power to consecrate the Body of Christ and to prepare the faithful for the reception of the Eucharist, which is the center of the whole Christian sacramental mystery. The power of Orders, we can also say, is the power of making Christ sacramentally present and active in the Church. Those who have received it in its plenitude, the Bishops, can transmit it either in its fullness, by consecrating other Bishops, or in part, by conferring Holy Orders. Among these latter, the priesthood and the deaconate are certainly also of divine institution. (We do not wish here to take sides in the question of ascertaining whether or not the Episcopacy constitutes, properly speaking, a superior order with relation to the priesthood.)

When they act in accordance with the power of Orders in administering the Sacraments, the members of the Hierarchy are the instruments of Christ, free, personal instruments, to the extent that the exercise of this power requires a free act on their part. A Sacrament is valid only if its minister consciously wants to administer it. Nevertheless, he is still only an instrument. It is Christ Who sanctifies by means of his ministry; through him, the faithful are put in contact with Christ.

The power of Orders was communicated to the Apostles by Christ with the fullness of the priesthood. All of them received it directly from Christ, and not through the intermediary of Peter. They transmitted it to their successors, the Bishops, and these can in turn transmit it also. They can do so licitly with the consent of the Pope; They can do so validly even against his will. It is thus that the schismatical churches can perpetuate in themselves the Episcopate and the priesthood. There is no superiority of the Pope over the Bishops from the point of view of the power of Orders taken in itself. A simple priest cannot ordain another priest, since he has not received the fullness of the priesthood. He cannot licitly make use of his power of Orders without the consent of his Bishop, but he can do so validly. He can always, no matter what his situation may be, celebrate Mass validly. The power of Orders has therefore as its end to insure our sanctification by Christ.

The Power of Jurisdiction. The third function of the Hierarchy is the government of the Church. That is assured by what is called the power of jurisdiction. This deals with the social relations of Christians as Christians. Its purpose is the proper organization of the visible Church, the proper conduct of the Church as the people of God living in earthly conditions. It is exercised either by means of general laws (which make up "Canon Law," the code of the Church), or by means of particular decisions. It pertains to the Hierarchy, by virtue of its power of jurisdiction, to adapt the laws of the Church to times and places, to take all the means necessary for discipline and good order. All the same, this power is not unlimited; it is exercised only within the limits set up by Christ. The Hierarchy cannot modify what is of divine institution in the makeup of the Church. In effect, it has received from Christ a power of jurisdiction in order to govern His Church during the time that His visible absence will continue, that is, as long as the world lasts.

The power of jurisdiction was given by Christ to

the Apostles, but dependent upon Peter. The Bishops possess it therefore only dependent on the Pope, which implies that a particular Bishop has no legitimate jurisdiction unless it be confided to him by the Pope who can take it away from him, and that the Pope always has the right to intervene directly in a diocese. Nevertheless, he cannot govern the Church without Bishops and they are not his delegates. It is not for reasons of mere practical convenience that there are Bishops—their existence in the Church is of divine right. But the Pope is superior to the Bishops from the point of view of jurisdiction. It is in virtue of his pre-eminent place in this regard that he is called the Vicar of Jesus Christ. He is not His successor, as though he took His place, but only His Vicar, the visible representative who governs in His name and by His actual, not past, authority. If there is at the head of the Church a Bishop, the Bishop of Rome, who has competence and authority not over just a portion of the Church, but over the whole Church, and is the only one to have it, the reason must not be sought primarily in the advantages of one-man rule; rather, it is in this way, in accordance with the Will of Christ, that the oneness of the Church and her invisible Head is visibly brought out.

It is well to insist on the difference of the relationship which the power of jurisdiction and the power of Orders each have to Christ. Through the power of Orders, the Hierarchy is an instrument of sanctification in the hands of Christ in the administration of the Sacraments; it places the acts through which the grace of Christ will flow. The power of jurisdiction also comes from Christ. The Hierarchy receives it within certain limits, since, as we have said, it cannot modify the divine constitution of the Church which assures her her place. But within these limits, it has full power to decide, and what it decides becomes for the faithful the Will of Jesus Christ Himself. There is no doubt that God gives His graces to those who are thus charged with commanding in His name; no doubt that He watches over the Church to the extent that she cannot disappear. The assistance of the Holy Spirit is promised her, and the preparing of the Kingdom of God will never cease being done through her. Our pastors will never render impossible the work they have the mission of promoting.

Nevertheless, Christ has not guaranteed that those whom He has set up in the Church will always make decisions which are objectively the wisest and best-suited; we need not create such an illusion in order to believe. Still, it is with reason that we admire Canon Law as being a marvelous work of wisdom. However, it is never claimed that all the desirable reforms have always been made as soon as it was opportune, and especially in the case of particular decisions, it is never claimed that they have always been or will always be the best possible.

But what we have to maintain is that when the Hierarchy gives us a command on its own ground which is that of the religious and moral life (later on we shall see how the temporal order can be affected indirectly), as long as the fulfilling of the order it gives does not constitute a sin, it expresses the Will of Christ for us. It is this Will of Christ that we are fulfilling by obeying it. Without a doubt there is a profound mystery in seeing Christ's all-holy Will thus hiding itself, so to speak, behind the imperfections and unavoidable insufficiencies

of His representatives. But we are not obliged any the
less to look for it where He has been pleased to put it,
to listen to it wherever He is pleased to express it, and
not where we would like to find it. We know that
Christ watches over His Church and will never allow
her to stop doing His work. We know that only in her
is the coming of the Kingdom being prepared. We
know that nothing is to be preferred to unity, the bonds
of which are loosened by all unruliness. By our obedience, we are contributing to the preparation of the Kingdom of God; by disobeying, we only hinder it. It is in
the power of jurisdiction, because the exercise thereof
involves the intervention of a larger share of what is
human, that Jesus Christ hides Himself more thoroughly
behind the Hierarchy He has instituted. But He is nonetheless present in it and acting through it. You see here
to what extent the Church is a human-divine mystery.
The divine makes use of the human, but it neither ab-
sorbs nor surpresses it.

This threefold function of the Hierarchy has as its
end the sanctification of souls. By their power of Magisterium, of Orders and of jurisdiction, the Apostles and
their successors bring about the perfection of the Mystical Body. Entrance into the Kingdom, the Coming of
the Kingdom is bound up with their ministry. It is not
a question simply of governing an earthly society, no
matter how august. In this also the visible and the invisible are united. That is why, too, that the Hierarchy
knows it has received its powers for the service and the
good of those whom it rules. One of the titles that the
Pope gives himself is that of *servus servorum Dei*. That
is not an honorific title. The members of the Hierarchy
consider themselves as bearers of the action of Christ.

They do not act by virtue of power which they have of themselves or which they merit by their personal qualities; it is Christ who wishes to make use of them to reach all the faithful.

Lastly, let us add that the exercise of these different powers is bound up with the state in which the Church finds herself on earth. There is no doubt that those who have received the Sacrament of Holy Orders will always remain Bishops or priests, since Orders impress a character. But at the end, in the state of perfection, the power of Teaching will no longer have any object, since vision will have succeeded Faith. The power of Orders will be superfluous, since we will be united directly, fully and without any veils to the Source of holiness. The power of jurisdiction will no longer be needed— there will no longer be any need for anyone to take the place of Christ Who will no longer be invisible, and it will be Charity in Light, which, possessed by all, will insure the unity, the cohesion of the Church. No longer will there be any need for a Law, for an external command, since the living Law, Charity, will have become internal to each one, and no one will ever be in danger of taking anything at all away from it in himself. Every veil will be lifted, all vicariousness abolished, all "pedagogies" by-passed, and there will be only "Christ, all in all."

8

The Position of the Christian
in the Church

The last time we spoke of the Hierarchy, we tried to
bring out the meaning of its function based entirely
on its relationship with Christ. But the Church is not
merely a Hierarchy, since the Hierarchy also exists for
the faithful. There is therefore the mass of the faithful.
In using this term mass, I do not wish to give it any
pejorative nuance. I just want to say that it is a matter
of large numbers. However, after having heard me insist so much on the Hierarchy and its powers, you are
under the impression, perhaps, that the faithful in the
Catholic Church are, as such, reduced to passivity. I say
"as such" because while it is true that the Hierarchy
commands only in the religious domain (or in what is
ultimately linked to this domain), there always remains
to the faithful the initiative in what is properly human,

for example, in professional activity. But still and all, does not the obedience which Catholics owe the Hierarchy reduce them to passivity in the religious life?

This is a reproach often leveled against the Catholic Church, and people add that in giving her subjects this passive attitude in the religious domain, the Church, given the unity of man, disposes them to carry over the same attitude everywhere else. Thus a Catholic formation would tend to make passive beings, shrunken beings, without breadth of vision, without initiative, with no awareness of their own responsibilities with regard to the great problems of life, always waiting for someone to command them, to tell them in every case what they are to think, and never looking beyond the particular task which is prescribed for them. It is possible that some Catholics may have given rise to this reproach— we may even say that it is certain. But let us add that in so doing they do not represent what the Church demands.

In the first place a Christian must not shut himself up in his particular task. Indeed, we can look upon the Church as a great body each of whose members has a special function in view of the good of the whole, and has the essential duty of carrying it out as best he can. But, as Pascal says, she is a body of "thinking members," that is, something quite different from a carnal organism; something quite other too than a machine, each of whose members has its role to play in the productions of the whole unit, but which nevertheless finds its true unity only in the mind of the one who sets the parts in motion. Though closely enmeshed with one another, these parts nevertheless remain foreign to one another because they are working together for the realization of a plan they do not know.

We however are capable by means of thought, of surpassing our own limitations and really associating ourselves with the common effort. Charity makes it a duty for us to do so. The Church is not only a body—she is a communion. Let us recall with St. John that Christians must, by means of their union with Christ, be united among themselves just as Christ is one with His Father. Each one has to bear within himself the knowledge and the love of the whole, as well as remain attentive to his concrete situation and give himself to his own task, so as to make in a conscious way, the contribution demanded of him. The entire Church must in this way be present in every Christian—must live in each Christian.

And that is but a consequence and an expression of the catholicity of the Church. If, as we have demonstrated, it is essential for her to bring back to unity the whole human diversity which she embraces, to bring it back to the highest form of unity, that which consists not only of cooperation in the same undertaking, but of a communion of spirits and hearts surpassing all human sentiment, then we are obliged by that fact to conform ourselves in spirit to her. There is nothing that is less in conformity with the spirit of true Christianity than a certain habit of shutting oneself up entirely in one's task, even with the sincere intention of carrying it out for the good of the whole. Therefore, the existence of a Hierarchy does not have for its purpose to distract us from thinking of the whole. It is set up to direct and harmonize efforts. While we must not wish to make decisions in the place of those who are charged with that, nor intervene indiscreetly in the work of another, it would be egoism and laziness disguised under the appearances of humility to declare that the problems of others are not our problems, that their concerns are not our concerns, that the situations in which we are not personally involved are so far beyond us that we need not preoccupy ourselves with them.

Of course, the lack of time, and often also the impossibility of getting information, limit us quite a bit. Nothing of value is accomplished without a certain concentration not only of forces but also of thought itself. Nevertheless, it remains that a Christian who is faithful to the spirit of the Church will, in the religious domain, have a feeling for the most universal views and preoccupations possible. It is a matter of attitude, a spontaneous openness, perfectly compatible with serious attentiveness to one's own business, even necessary in order to avoid a certain narrowness in carrying it on. Now it is perfectly correct to say that everyone tends to carry over into everything dispositions acquired in one particular domain. The result is that even in purely human affairs, no one will show himself to be further removed from the meanness of those whose views are narrow and whose horizons are limited than the true Christian. Certainly we must not believe that we have the mission of governing the Church, or even of counseling those who govern her. But let us not say of any Christian problem: that does not concern me since there is a Hierarchy to be concerned with it and straighten it out. Though it is the Hierarchy's job to decide on the solution to a problem, that does not alter the fact that we will not be fully Christian unless the problem has stirred something in us.

However, we are speaking here of a preoccupation, a participation of the heart which doubtless tears away at egoism and narrowness but which is not in the order of action. Must we then let people say that the Catholic has a passive role in his Church? No. To understand this, it helps to understand that dependence on the Hierarchy may take two quite distinct forms. According to the first, which is the most commonly envisaged, the initiative comes from higher up, in the form of an order to be carried out. Even in this case we must be careful not to believe that there is just passivity on the part of the one who executes the order. The order has to be understood not only in its materiality, so to speak, but also in its orientation and in its complete context, so that it may be carried out in the best possible way. Unintelligent executors, those who did not want to take the trouble to understand, are false to the intention of the one who gives the order, and no one would try to pass that off as a perfection of obedience. Moreover, while the order fixes a goal to be attained, it does not determine all the concrete means; that is generally impossible to do because it is only on the spot and at the moment of execution, as it unfolds, that a situation can be precisely evaluated. An intelligent authority therefore leaves some initiative, some choice, some responsibility to the executor within the framework of the orders given. In short, a man, in a dependence of this sort, is treated not as an instrument but as a free and reasonable person. Still we have to recognize that the initiative which sets the executor's initiative in motion is outside of him and places limits on him.

There is a second form of dependence upon the Hierarchy—one in which the initiative comes from the subject, the Hierarchy's role being then to control, to judge the work undertaken or terminated, either to approve and accept it, or to reject it. Again, it is a matter of a decision which would be imposed. But, though it comes in second place and manifests itself in the form of a judgment and not of a command, the intervention of the Hierarchy demands just as much obedience.

Of course, the first of these two forms exists in the Church. It is manifested, we have said, either by means of general rules or by particular commands. Within the limits fixed by Jesus Christ Himself, which no one consequently can either extend or restrict, the Hierarchy has the right to command every time it sees fit to do so. It is not a matter then of eliminating or reducing in any way this first kind of dependence. But nothing is detracted from it if we say that alongside of it, the second form of dependence has a place in every society. Though there are societies wherein the first of the two would be sufficient to assure life and progress, I will limit myself to noting merely that this second form of dependence also exists in the Church. If it is true that the Christian must always act in the way the Hierarchy points out to him, it does not follow that he can or must act only when an order is given him. Of course, his action would always have to be subject to the judgment of the Hierarchy which might either approve it in a tacit or a formal way, or else censure it. And the acceptance of this judgment, whatever it be, is a duty of obedience.

Authority in the Church is therefore not the only source of initiative and movement. The reason is that Christ diffuses His Spirit throughout the whole Body of His Church, and that His inspirations can attain each faithful person directly. In this, it is necessary to be precise, so as not to expose ourselves to falling into error. No member of the Church (this we have already said, though not in so many words) can avail himself of an interior inspiration to go against a decision of authority (I am pre-supposing that the latter is commanding on its own terrain and is not ordering what would be sinful); for lawful authority speaks in the name of Christ, and there can be no contradiction between what Christ ordains and what He inspires by means of His Spirit.

On the other hand, we are always in danger of confusing the inspiration that comes from the Spirit with ideas which spring from ourselves—expressions in the religious sphere of our own temperament, of our human aspirations. The control exercised by the Hierarchy is a means of telling the two apart. It is certain that going against a decision of the Hierarchy is not a way of giving greater obedience to the inspirations of the Spirit. No one therefore can ever presume upon inspiration to disobey. But, having brought this out, (we can say)* that the Spirit can invite the faithful to action, orient them toward definite tasks without going through the channels of authority; for He is sent to the whole Church.

There is room, therefore, a great deal of room, in the Christian's life, for initiative which at its source is independent of the Hierarchy. Still, from another point of view, even this initiative is obedience—it must seek to be obedience to the Holy Spirit. The most sincerely and completely submissive Christian need not remain passive, always waiting for a sign from the authorities before undertaking a project. He can—we may even say he must—ask himself what he can do, in what way he can give something to the Church, or contribute to the solution of one of the many kinds of problems that come up before her. He has to have the courage to go ahead on

* Parenthetical explanation mine.

his own responsibility, always being ready to accept in a filial spirit the decisions of the Hierarchy as soon as they become known.

When we look at the history of the Church, we see how many important, nay essential things, owe their existence to the initiative—afterwards ratified by the Hierarchy—of simple laymen. And at the same time, we see how the vigilance and intervention of the Hierarchy are necessary in order to separate the cockle or at least the straw from the good grain, and what disorders would inevitably have resulted if free rein had been given to individual inspirations. The Church has constantly been enriched by a multitude of projects which the Hierarchy eventually controlled, which it sometimes straightened out before accepting, but which it had not begun.

Let us take a few examples from different domains. People often point to the transformation of piety toward Christ that manifested itself in the 12th and 13th centuries (cf. *Christus, La Religion chretienne*, pp. 1152-1153). That was due in part to the monastic influence. But it is clear that its origin did not lie in a pre-conceived plan and that it was not accomplished on order. The new sentiments which saw the light of day were first of all the expression of an individual piety that was passed on from person to person. Prayers as popular and may we say as official—in the sense that they are recognized, encouraged, recommended by the Hierarchy—as the Rosary, were also born of individual initiative. The same should be said for devotions like the Way of the Cross or the Sacred Heart. From time to time, the Church condemns devotions or practices which seek to spread. In this way selectivity is introduced. But the great Catholic devotions were not imposed by authority nor created as whole entities. The Hierarchy merely consecrated what had sprung up among the masses of the faithful, once it had recognized therein the authentic inspiration of the Spirit. Faithful souls would have had a poor understanding of their duty if they had imagined that they had to await an order or some sort of invitation to give such and such a form to their devotion.

Passing on to a different field, we might mention the intellectual efforts of St. Thomas Aquinas. When he began his work, the introduction of Aristotelianism in the learned circles of Christianity had not been accorded a very favorable reception on the part of the ecclesiastical authority. Warnings and even condemnations had not been lacking. Yet St. Thomas did not think he was being disobedient when, following in the footsteps of his teacher, Albert, he patiently took up a word that had gotten off to a bad start from the outset. We know how much the Church has since eulogized him. Here then is another project, and one of immense significance, which was not undertaken on request of the Hierarchy but upon personal initiative, and against many obstacles. It can be attributed to an inspiration of the Spirit, but this inspiration was not produced in an extraordinary way. It utilized the calm reflections of a religious on the needs of the Church in his time.

We may also cite a series of events as important in the life of the Church as the founding of the religious orders. The Hierarchy did not raise them up. All of them came about as a result of the initiative of one or several members of the Church who, based on the conditions of their times, understood the necessity for a new institution adapted to this or that need, who saw the project to its realization (often as first by trial and error, without seeing just where the Holy Spirit was leading them) in the face of innumerable difficulties, and caused it to be progressively approved. From among so many examples, we shall briefly call to mind the reform of Carmel by St. Teresa, because admirable accounts (*Life* by herself, and *Foundations*) allow us to follow it in detail. No one had given her the mission to do that. At the outset, it was not the encouragement of her superiors that pushed her on, and the permissions she banked on were not forthcoming as rapidly as she might have wished. Not a single case of disobedience to orders received can be found in her life—one single case where she might have gone beyond the limits set for her. But never did she get discouraged about it either. She did not wait to be understood to start things going; she did not use coldness or opposition as an excuse to abandon her task. She tried hard to convince, she used to the full all the liberties she was allowed. And to the greater service of the Church and the profound success of the Catholic rebirth, she succeeded at last. She serves as an example of a close union of the most loyal obedience and the most enterprising initiative. It will be said that we are using an exceptional personality as an example. No doubt. But each Christian in his own sphere, with his own means, must imitate *pro modulo suo* this kind of initiative and obedience. A multitude of particular efforts is no less indispensable nor less fruitful than the exceptional action of several powerful personalities.

Initiative, as we have said, must at no time either go against a decision already taken, or correct the judgment of the Hierarchy when it makes a pronouncement. Indeed we must always act for the good of the Church, for the advancement of the Kingdom of God. But one is not seconding the designs of Christ when one disobeys those to whom He has confided the power of commanding in His name. On this point, a Catholic would not think of agreeing to either exception or compromise. No objection of conscience is valid against the Church. No matter how convinced a person may be of the necessity of the project undertaken, no matter how persuaded that it serves the interests of Christ, that person will not pursue it against the manifest will of the Church. Still, this absolute need for submissiveness is justified only in the light of the Catholic doctrine on the Hierarchy. If we see in the Church only a human society, no matter how venerable, how tried and time-tested, how far-seeing she may be, we cannot recognize her right to exact this unconditional obedience. That is the reason why those unbelievers who have exalted the concept of authority and discipline in the Church while reducing her to a mere human institution, were able to do so only by underestimating the value of the person. Unless the ecclesiastical authority speaks in the name of Jesus Christ Himself, its empire over the faithful is tyrannical in the true sense of the word.

But, although for a Catholic there can be no question of revising the judgment of the Church, still he must be able to measure its scope so as to understand what it is she demands. As long as she has given no unalterable decision in a matter of faith or morals, it is permissible respectfully to seek, with sufficient reason, to bring the representatives of the Hierarchy to review positions they have taken. This must never take on the aspect of a protest, still less of agitation in the public forum. But by addressing oneself directly to them, it is possible to present certain new facets of the problem and explain the reasons which seem to require a different solution.

It must be added that a good number of the most absolute decisions are of a negative nature. They block off a route that could only lead to error or to evil, but they do not delineate the only possible path along which research might be profitable. They do not therefore necessarily signify—far from it—that one must throw himself back purely and simply on previous positions. There again, if the revolt is a culpable one, the most perfect thing would not of necessity be to retire into one's shell and maintain silence. There could be in this attitude more spite and pride than true submissiveness. It might be better to take up the work again while taking into account the light shed by the condemnation, with a view to arriving at a new result that the Church could approve and that would redound to her benefit. Let us note in passing that it is a relatively recent—and unjustified—state of mind that causes a man to be considered as disqualified for further research when he has once had to be disapproved.

The initiative accorded the Christian is therefore not a concession to his need for independence, as though it were a certain leeway given him so as not to be asking too much from him. Not at all. It is required of him. He has to place himself at Christ's service as much by his initiative as by his dependence. It is a fault not to want to submit oneself to given orders; it is also a fault not to want to undertake what one is capable of doing in and for the Church. This latter fault is perhaps less visible, less capable of being pin-pointed than the former, so to speak, and attracts less attention. It belongs to that category of faults of omission that we are too prone to consider as nothing, and that the Gospel of the Talents should make us consider serious. Whether it be inspired by laziness and lack of concern or by pusillanimity, by a fear of responsibility, this attitude of always awaiting a request by the Hierarchy before getting into action is not Christian.

There is a domain in which Christian initiative is particularly necessary, especially on the part of lay Christians; and that is when there is question of discovering, of devising means of translating the demands of Christian doctrine into social, political, economic actions. There above all the role of the Hierarchy will not be to dictate solutions in advance, but to control, to distinguish, and to rectify those which Christian laymen have worked out—to restrain solutions that are too inadequate, to point out elements of doctrine that seem to have been forgotten, etc. And it is in those times when the world is in transformation, when living conditions are being renovated at a stepped-up pace, that the activity of the Christian is more indispensable than ever.

It happens that some Christians complain that the Church seems "behind the times," that the initiative has been left to unbelievers. And they are tempted to turn to the Hierarchy with reproaches. The first question they ought to ask themselves is whether these reproaches do not rather fall upon them. Have not they or their elders remained inert, waiting for some-sort of a push (pre-supposing that they are really ready to act upon it) when it was up to them to act, to search? They should at least have made some attempts on which a judgment could have been made, which could have been criticized or encouraged, and in this way, the needed adaptation could have begun . . .

This is by way of saying that initiative on the part of Christians is a normal element in the life of the Church. When it is lacking, one of the functions of the Church is not guaranteed, and the action of the Hierarchy, no matter how vigilant, cannot make up for it completely. You see sufficiently well now how it would be an unjust reproach of Christianity to say that it favors passivity. It runs up against lack of discipline, laziness and the fear of responsibility, each in its turn, but it repudiates all of them.

A word remains to be said about the dispositions a Christian must maintain within himself so as to be in condition to acquit himself well of his duty of taking the initiative. First of all, it is obviously necessary to take all possible steps to insure that this initiative be a happy one and that it follow from the first, if possible, a course that the Church could approve. The only way to do this (we are not speaking here of those elements of the purely human order that would also have to be considered) is that it be undertaken as much as possible under the influence of the Spirit which animates the Christian. And the Spirit never ceases inspiring us, pushing us along the right path. If we go astray, it is because the voice of our egoism and of our self-love gets mixed up with His and drowns it out. It is because we mistake what stems from our sinful hearts for the inspiration of the Spirit. There is always the need, therefore, for a continuous purification, an ever-deeper detachment, an ever more delicate spiritual sensitivity (all of which requires assiduous prayer).

If we wish to act properly—and we must act, we do not have the right to take refuge in abstention—we must be ready to accept all eventual decisions of the Church concerning our actions, no matter how painful they may be. Otherwise, what is at the outset the most generous of initiatives would risk entailing rebellion later on. It is indeed easier to remain obedient when we wait passively for a push without having tried anything at all beforehand, than to renounce at the request of some authority, what we have undertaken: by the sheer weight of events, we have become attached to it, we have put our whole heart in it, just as in everything we have spent ourselves for.

It is always hard to admit that one has been wrong, and all the more so if one were sincerely aiming at the good of the Church and not personal advantage. On the other hand, a public disavowal is always a bit humiliating. Opponents one had run up against and who were probably also in serious error, or who had not always been disinterested, sometimes triumph without any qualms whatever. In short, when one has had the courage to undertake something, he may find obedience a difficult trial. One has to be able not only to submit, to resist the temptation to rebel, but also to do it without allowing oneself to become bitter, without letting it become a source of interior poisoning that afterwards makes life sterile. To hold out, therefore, it is necessary to have a strong spiritual life. But once again, it is necessary that each in his own sphere, according to his capacity, use some initiative. The good of the Kingdom of God demands it. And there is also a duty to acquire the virtues which will render one capable of doing so without suffering damage.

9

cf SCCTSD Proceedings 1961
also art by Weigel in Thom Reader

The Catholic Church and
Separated Churches

I. *Purpose of this study*

"The Separated Churches," "dissident Christians," "our separated brethren"—these are different expressions by which we designate the same fact. They are not all equally appropriate, but it is enough for us to understand that they remind us that outside the Catholic Church there are men who, like us, claim to be Christ's, who not only admire Him as an exceptional man, as the apex of our humanity, but who recognize in Him God come to earth to save us, who therefore see in Him the definitive revelation of God, after which none other is to be expected.

We may consider the same fact from another angle. In the course of history, small groups of men, without wishing to separate themselves from Christ, became separated from the Catholic Church to form outside of her, religious institutions which claim to be faithful—more faithful, to the true Christian past and to the real thought of Christ, institutions which believe that they are the depositaries of His message and that they continue His work.

Surely the existence of one single man outside the Church will always be a source of sorrow for a true Catholic, and this sorrow will not remain sterile, since it will be a source of prayer and of apostolate. But the existence outside the Church of important groups which claim to be Christ's causes this Catholic sorrow of a particular nature, and the duty of apostleship that results takes on a particular form in his case. Of course, one can, and should, try to bring back individually to the service of the Church souls that have wandered away from her— provided, naturally, that everything be done with sincerity, and that no questionable technique of proselytizing be employed. But since these cases concern Christians who have become incorporated into religious institutions, who are organized among themselves, who form a body, may we not in addition and above all, strive for the accomplishment of a much vaster task, namely, the reunion with the true Church of these dissident Christian organizations?

In this matter, you see, there are both a fact and a problem that are extremely complex, for the Christian status, if we may speak thus, of the "separated Churches" is far from being the same. That which separates them from the Catholic Church varies a great deal. We are not pretending today to treat the question in a complete, nor even a summary fashion, nor yet to bring out the known facts in all their complexity. Nor do I wish to state the conditions under which reunion would be possible, nor what are the means of arriving at that or at least of smoothing the way, for in the last analysis that can be the task of God alone. My only ambition is to interest you in this fact and this problem, to make it enter your circle of interests, and to indicate in a few words the fundamental attitude of mind and of life which can at least favor a happy solution. As a matter of fact, it is your duty to be preoccupied with it, because the Church is preoccupied with it, and that is enough to keep any true Christian from being indifferent to it. Besides, it could very well be that indifference is the most serious obstacle to the realization of the ardent wish, let us say hope even of the Church. That would be a fault against Charity.

II. *The main separations*

There were, then, in the course of history, fragments of the Christian world that became separated from the center of Catholic unity on questions of dogma or of discipline, while wishing to preserve the true doctrine of Christ and each claiming to be the real heir to the foundation made by Christ. Separation on a question of dogma is heresy. Separation on a point of discipline is schism. In practice there are no groups of dissident Christians living apart from the Church for purely disciplinary reasons. For all of them there is at least some point of dogma in dispute. But the importance of the dogmatic factor varies greatly, and from this point of view there is no comparison between what is called the Orthodox Church and Protestantism.

Let us first of all recall to mind what the principal separations were.

During the 5th century, as an aftermath of the Christ-ological discussions of the two Councils of Ephesus and of Chalcedon, the Nestorians, then the Monophysites, became separated. The Nestorians (so called after Nestorius, Patriarch of Constantinople whose exact teaching is still today the object of discussion among historians) refused to accept the doctrine of the unity of person in Christ (to speak rather schematically). The Monophysites, on the contrary, refused to accept the definition of the Council of Chalcedon on the retaining of a human nature in Christ without confusion with the divine nature. In reality, there was perhaps no real doctrinal divergence on their part, but they rejected the formula of faith which the Council of Chalcedon judged indispensable for the correct and unabridged statement of the doctrine.

The center of the Nestorian Church was initially Persia. It experienced a great development until the 13th century; it must not be forgotten that it evangelized Tartary, Mongolia, China (famous inscription of Singan-Fu), and certain parts of India. Today the Nestorians number only around 100,000. The Monophysite schism (perhaps we should speak rather of "monoenergism" than of "monophysism") found its adherents in Syria and Egypt, whence it reached Abyssinia. The statistics at the present time are, approximately: Armenians, 2,300,000; Jacobite Syrians, 80,000; Coptic Church (Egypt), 700,000; Church of Abyssinia, 3,500,000.

The most serious schism was that of Byzantium, because it resulted in the separation of almost all of the East, of everything that lived under the religious ascendancy of the great capital. After an initial schism in the days of the Patriarch Photius, union was re-established. But in 1054, Michael Cerularius broke it up again. Twice, at the Councils of Lyons (1274) and of Florence (1438), union was re-established, but it was ephemeral. The Orthodox Church is composed of "auto-cephalic" churches; that is, each one having its own particular religious organization by nationality possessing full autonomy with respect to the others, but all equally subject to the same invisible Head, Christ. The Patriarch of Constantinople has nonetheless retained a primacy of honor. These Churches number about 168,000,000 faithful, of whom 125,000,000 are Russian (it must be recognized however that a goodly number of the latter belong to sects which became detached from the common trunk, especially in the 17th century). There is an autonomous Russian Church in North America which numbers 250,000 faithful; there is an Orthodox Archbishopric in Japan which numbers 35,000. We must not fail to recognize the great racial and cultural diversity which is encountered in this enormous bloc of Orthodox Churches. (We are not speaking here of the dechristianization of a part of these masses, especially in Russia).

Then, in the 16th century came the great rupture of Protestantism. Its first protagonist was Luther, who drew the Germanic countries with him; then the influence of Calvin made itself felt especially in France, and that of Zwingli in Switzerland. In England, the separation which took place under the direction of Henry VIII was at first simply a schism. The Church of England broke with Rome and the king was her head; but a little later, notably under Edward VI, Lutheran elements were introduced into the faith and worship.

By reason of the principle of free search and the absence of a living doctrinal authority which could interpret the Bible, Protestantism broke up quite rapidly into a multitude of particular sects, and in each of the religious groups that issued from the Reformation, very divergent opinions are found. It is thus that in Anglicanism there is a High Church whose faith and worship are at times very close to those of the Catholic Church, alongside of currents where a much more radical Protestantism is manifest.

The lack of doctrinal authority has meant that the ravages of "modernism" were very severe, so much so that it may be asked at times, regarding this or that sect, what does remain of Christianity, of faith properly so-called? What is understood by "liberal Protestantism" is not so much a group apart as a current circulating among the most diverse groups. It scarcely comprises more than a religious philosophy according to which Christ is but a man who has achieved the highest of religious experiences. For liberal Protestantism, dogma has scarcely any significance any longer.

Approximately 209,000,000 men claim to be Protestants. Of this number, about half belong to non-conformist sects which became detached from the great primitive movements. The Anglican Church numbers from 30 to 32 million faithful, of whom 20 million are in England. There are 41 million Lutherans, the great majority of whom are in Germany. Thirteen million are spiritual heirs of Calvin and Zwingli. These figures have whatever value is attachable to religious statistics. To state precisely what their significance is would be a big job. (On this subject, with regard to Catholicism, see the work of G. Le Bras on religious practice in France).

Finally we might mention a group of Jansenists in

Holland; the "Old Catholics" in Germany, Switzerland and Austria, who refused to recognize the infallibility of the Pope, (about 30,000); a national Church in the Philippines (separated in 1902), 1,500,000 (?); the Czechoslovakian national Church, separated in 1920, about 650,000; the "German Catholics" separated in 1844, are in the process of disappearing.

III. *Catholic Elements in the diverse Confessions*

What the various branches separated from Catholic unity have preserved of the treasure of the Church varies a great deal from one to the other. In Protestantism, there remains the Bible as the Word of God. (Wherever the Bible is only considered as a human book, even if regarded as being the expression of the most elevated "religious experience," one can no longer speak of Christianity properly so-called). The fact that the Bible can only be interpreted authentically by the Magisterium, as we believe, does not mean that the Bible does not contain within itself the Word of God, to which the Church Herself is subject. The Magisterium merely interprets it, that is, gives it its true meaning. In preserving the Bible, the Protestants, are therefore keeping some thing authentically Christian. Of course the true meaning of the book is in part closed to them, despite the fervor, even the exclusivism of their love for it, or the zeal with which they study it. But this imperfect possession is for all that not without some fruit.

All the Protestant Confessions do not have Baptism. Only those who have preserved the rite fixed by Christ have kept it—though they are the most important ones; as long as it is administered with the intention of doing what Christ demands, it is valid. The confessions that have Baptism have at the same time Matrimony: every marriage of a baptized person is in fact a sacrament; the priest is an indispensable witness but only for Catholics as prescribed in Canon Law.

Leo XIII in his Apostolic Letter *Apostolicae curae* of September 13, 1896, adopted as his own the conclusion reached by the commission of theologians named by himself, refusing to recognize the validity of Anglican orders. Of course, this decision does not have the infallible stamp on it but it nevertheless does have a very serious import. (Some pastors have had themselves ordained by Jansenist or Old Catholic Bishops).

Dogmatic divergencies among Protestants are considerable from one confession to another (and often within the same confession). A part of Anglicanism, the Anglo-Catholics (its best known representative is Lord Halifax who took part in the conversations of Malines organized by Cardinal Mercier) does not differ very much from Catholicism from the point of view of faith, except as regards the place to be assigned to the Pope in the Church. But even in Anglicanism there is no real doctrinal homogeneity.

The Orthodox Churches are in an entirely different situation. A certain number of doctrinal divergencies can be noted between them and us. Regarding the procession of the Holy Spirit in the interior of the Trinity, we say: "ex Patre Filioque" or "ex Patre per Filium," whereas the Orthodox say simply: "ex Patre," and some of their theologians force this contrast so as to draw from it all sorts of antithetical consequences. In the matter of sacraments, the "character" in Holy Orders and Confirmation seems to be unknown; the essence of Matrimony is placed in the blessing of the priest and not in the contract between baptized persons; the moment of Consecration, in the Mass, is localized at the "epiclesis," the invocation to the Holy Spirit which follows the repetition of the words of the Last Supper. The Immaculate Conception is not universally admitted, though devotion to the Blessed Virgin is very deep and plays a major part in their Worship. Purgatory seems to be rejected, but that is possibly a matter of explanations. Finally, certain ones do not admit the complete possession of God by the purified soul prior to the Last Judgment. But there is above all the question of the primacy and infallibility of the Roman Pontiff. This is the most serious matter. It seems that, if that were settled, there would be no insurmountable difficulties in coming to an agreement on the other questions.

The Orthodox possess Baptism and all the Sacraments (despite the partial errors pointed out regarding some of them, errors which have not entailed the alteration of prescribed rites). There is therefore an apostolic succession in the Episcopacy, since the Bishops are validly consecrated; they possess, in consequence, the power of Orders in its fullness. So well does the Catholic Church recognize the reality of this power of Orders in the Orthodox Churches that she allows the faithful, in the event of danger of death, if there is no Catholic priest to whom recourse may be had, to ask an Orthodox priest for the Sacraments (Penance, the Eucharist, Extreme-Unction), provided the danger of scandal be avoided. There is, finally, an ascetic and spiritual tradition in Orthodoxy that contains numerous elements of great value. Pius XI said on this subject, in an address before Italian university students, on January 9, 1927: "Not enough is known about all that is precious, good, Christian, in the remnants of ancient Catholic truth. Pieces broken off from gold-bearing rock also contain some gold. The ancient Christianities of the Orient have preserved such real holiness that they deserve not only respect but our entire sympathy."

And the Catholic Church has always made a great distinction in her manner of handling the Orthodox and the Protestants. In official documents, the term "churches" is applied to the Orthodox confessions which on the other hand are not called "orthodox," something that is not done for the Protestant confessions. Moreover, the Church has always sought reunion as a body with them—that is, collective reconciliation, when dealing with their Hierarchies. They are treated as real ecclesiastical bodies unfortunately cut off from the Catholic communion, but having kept in spite of everything a real consistency of apostolic origin. The reconciliations that have taken place (whether ephemeral and with the whole of Orthodoxy, as at the Councils of Lyons and Florence, or lasting, and with groups generally not considerable in size) have been truly reunions as a body and not merely a sum of individual conversions. This stems from the homogeneity of the Orthodox confessions as ecclesiastical bodies; it stems also from all that they keep intact both of Christian doctrine and of sacramental realities.

IV. *This state of separation must be felt to be a scandal*

It must be considered in that way by all who have the Spirit of Christ—therefore, by Catholics. The fact is that Jesus Christ came on earth to accomplish a work of unity. He came, as St. John says, "to bring together all the children of God who were scattered." On the eve of His death (end of the discourse after the Last Supper) He prayed for the unity of His disciples. It is of course a source of grief to see men, no matter who they may be, outside the bonds of unity. But it is a source of greater grief to see those who claim to be Christ's, those who proclaim themselves to be and want to be His disciples, separated, opposed to one another. It is an object of scandal for non-Christians. Think of what the spectacle of our divisions must evoke in them . . .

Let us not attempt to throw the entire responsibility on the other confessions by saying that they were wrong to become separated. Without any doubt they were wrong to break up the unity. As we have said, there never is any valid reason for leaving the Catholic Church, because it is from her that we can and must obtain the remedy for the insufficiencies and evils we find in her. But that does not alter the fact that those who remained in the Church were in the wrong too. In fact, many of them were in the wrong. By their inadequacies, or by their scandalous conduct, or by pride-inspired pretentions, or by indifference or lack of charity, they contributed to pushing their brethren to revolt. It is always wrong to follow bad example; but the one who gives it has committed the first fault, and he will be held accountable also for the fault of his imitator. In like manner, if it is wrong to leave the Church, it is no less a fault to drive someone to it, one might almost say, in certain specific cases, to back one's neighbor into a corner, by the unchristian way one behaves toward him. History must not be made partial for apologetic ends. Nor must we, in false generosity, when looking for the reason for certain schisms, place all the faults on the side of the Catholics. Besides, we are not required to make up an impossible balance sheet. It is sufficient for us to know, and history attests to this, that there have been faults on our part too, to feel a bitter regret for them and to reproach ourselves with them before God.

If now we look at things in the present, we must not crush those who still do not see that the fullness of truth resides in the Catholic Church. What St. Augustine said applies to many of those who belong to the other Christian confessions: "Those who while propounding a false and corrupt dogma nevertheless do not adhere to it in a spirit of partiality, especially when, far from having through prideful presumption taken the initiative in the error, but having inherited it from parents who were first its victims, they themselves, disposed to straighten themselves out once they have found it, ardently seek the truth: those must not be considered heretics" (Letter 43, n. 2). They may be called heretics materially, since on such and such a point they profess error; they are heretics juridically in some sort, since they belong to a heretical confession; but such they are not in themselves, in the depths of their hearts, in their wills, since they are disposed to recognize the truth if it manifests itself. That is what St. Augustine means.

Among all those who are separated from us are found not only men who are outside of the unity through their own fault; far from it. The majority have never personally committed an act of heresy or of schism; most have never even thought of it. And moreover, are there not in us, actually, in our personal attitudes, many things which make it more difficult for them to believe that we dwell in the truth? Do we do nothing that is of such a nature as to reinforce some of their prejudices? Do we cause the truth confided to us to glow brilliantly? Have we even been interested in them? Do we have an ardent desire, without any admixture of too-human views, to see them return to the fold? Is there something lacking to us as long as they are outside? If we cannot give a satisfactory answer to all these questions—and who would dare say without pharisaism that he has nothing to reproach himself with in all this?—we have to consider this abiding separation as something which involves our responsibility. We have our share of culpability in the scandal of disunity.

These days, a call to union has been heard from the non-Catholic camp; a call in which the action of the Holy Spirit can legitimately be recognized. On the Catholic side, a very marked effort is taking shape to know the non-Catholic confessions better, not only in their history and organization, but in that which they may possess of spiritual riches, in what they have preserved of the Christian heritage. There are also initiatives like those of the Conversations of Malines, in 1921, 1923, and 1925 between Catholics and Anglicans, led respectively by Cardinal Mercier and Lord Halifax. These were of a private character and were aimed chiefly at making the respective positions better known. It would take too long to try to inventory them; they were delicate things which cannot be resumed in a few words.

Among non-Catholics, the desire for the union of all Christians has been felt as much by the Orthodox as by the Protestants. This desire has given rise to a movement called "Ecumenism," a movement that has taken on vast proportions and has spread more and more in those circles where faith is most lively and religious life most intense. Unfortunately the doctrine which sustains it suffers from the inadequacies, the errors, also the diversity of the teachings about the Church that prevail in the non-Catholic confessions. Of course, it is normal for the idea that is formed about the conditions and means of union to vary according to the idea of the Church one is trying to bring about. Depending on what the latter is to be, men will make different judgments both about the present situation they are starting from and about the situation they are tending toward.

We cannot examine these different doctrines. We will merely say a word about the position of the Catholic Church with respect to union. The Catholic Church obviously cannot allow that she be asked to adhere to another confession which would be considered as the true Church of Jesus Christ. Besides, it can be said that none of the partisans of the ecumenical movement present the matter in that way. But another idea is found—with various modifications, among practically all of them. No existing confession, it is said, is actually the Church. Each has preserved some Christian values which it must put into a common fund with the others. The Church in her fullness will therefore result from the reunion of the diverse Christian confessions which are today separated. Now the Catholic Church cannot accept this point of view either. She knows that she is the true Church of Christ, heiress of His promises. The dogma she teaches cannot be questioned. The essential organization she received from Christ cannot be modified. On the other hand, in those portions of her discipline which are of human institution, she could lend herself to adaptations that would not run counter to the good of souls. The differences in matters of law and liturgy that exist between eastern and western Christianities within the bosom of Catholic unity are a good demonstration of the breadth of spirit of the Church. She does not consider the mission she has received of continuing Christ and transmitting His message down through the generations as a privilege on which she could pride herself, but as a deposit which was confided to her, for which she bears the responsibility. That is what explains her intransigence. That must not be taken as the attitude of someone defending his rights, his advantages, his privileges, who refuses all concessions, who always wants the sacrifices demanded by a reconciliation to be at someone else's expense. No. She defends the divine truth to which she is humbly subject, and she cannot allow anyone to cast a slur upon it, or even put it up for discussion. While doing so, far from opposing unity, she serves it and makes it possible.

For it is not a question of obtaining human unity which might be a matter of compromise between opposing claims. It is a question of becoming re-united in Christ, of becoming re-united in His truth. In maintaining firmly that which is the visible Body of Christ on earth, one preserves for the future the chance of a reunion of some value. If by some impossibility the Catholic Church were to make some concessions on any point of her dogma or of her divine constitution, all hope of a real reunion would disappear, because with an alteration in His Body, Christ would cease to be present on earth. But we know that the Church is kept from such failings, and that in this way the Body of Christ will always be maintained, where Christians who found themselves dispersed will be able to become re-united.

But while the Catholic Church thus believes that she is the true Church and the sole legitimate heir of Christ, she does not for all that deny that there are in the other confessions many authentic though confused Christian riches which can be lived therein with remarkable intensity. Also, on one hand we are assured that reunion will be a great good for the separated confessions, for it will give them all that they lack by re-attaching them to the sole Body of Christ, but we recognize on the other hand that this reunion will be a great good, a source of new wealth, for the Catholic Church herself. Not that the Church, speaking absolutely, lacks any essential Christian value; but all Christians do not live all of them with the same intensity—not by any manner of means. Now, the reunion of separated confessions could have as an effect, let us say that it would normally have as an effect, to cause the values preserved in these confessions to be lived more intensely in Catholic unity. In coming back to the Church, they will keep whatever they have that is positive, whatever is legitimate in the spiritual temperament and the religious aspirations that are a partial explanation for them; they will have to renounce only their partialities, their narrowness, in short all that is negative in them and a cause of error for them. Thanks to what they bring, reunion will be for the Church the means of making her catholicity more real—not of becoming more Catholic: that she is already in her essence which requires nothing more nor less; but of making what she is more manifest, of placing her universal nature in greater relief and to greater advantage (cf. Congar, *Chretiens desunis*, pp. 316 et sq.).

Such enrichment would extend to every Christian, since every Christian participates in the whole Church. In this way again, you can see that we are not dealing with a human work, founded on a compromise wherein each sacrifices something, but rather with an assent, under the prompting of the Holy Spirit, to the whole truth, on the part of those who possessed truths that were only partial and more or less deformed; an assent which at the same time makes for a better understanding, a greater penetration, of the whole truth on the part of those who, in principle, already possess it. "I was kept," Newman wrote, "in one or the other of these (religious) sections or divisions, for a certain time, then I passed on to another, then to another. But in so doing, I lost nothing, in the end, of what I had at the outset. The positive truths of the Gospel have always dwelt within me. In my passage I have let fall negations, and it is only in this way that one of the phases of my religious life differed from the others."

10

The Church and the Salvation of Non-Believers

I. *The Church—sole means of salvation*

In speaking of the importance of the Church question, we said from the first that she was the sole means of salvation. That is indeed her essential affirmation regarding herself. She has always had and expressed this conviction. She has always seen something essential in it, because it is directly linked to that other essential truth that there is no salvation except through Christ. In fact, Christ is only possessed in and through the Church. A person cannot communicate with Christ without belonging to the Church. We have said it often enough: the Church—and we always understand by that the Catholic Church, visible, hierarchic—is the only living environment wherein one may be united to Christ and participate in His life. Such is, we say, her most profound reality, which the man who has only seen her from the outside has not grasped. He still does not know her. The necessity of belonging to the Church derives then from that in her which is the most profound. If the Church is the Body of Christ, we can only repeat with St. Augustine: "If you wish to live by the Spirit of Christ, you must live in the Body of Christ." Therefore one must neither separate himself from the Church nor remain outside her fold.

Already in the 3rd century, in St. Cyprian, are found famous formulas which do not express merely his particular opinion, since the Church herself ratified them and made them hers: "He who wants to have God for a Father must have the Church for a Mother"; "No one can be saved outside the Church," or this briefer one, which has been the most frequently retained: "Outside the Church there is no salvation."

II. *The problem of the non-believers*

But now a problem arises. Is that not a condemnation of so many unbelievers, of non-Catholics, of so many who have lived outside the Church? It is an immense problem; a problem that is not merely speculative, that does not arise from the need of harmonizing conflicting statements, but spontaneously from our Charity toward men, our brethren, a problem to which it is not possible, therefore, for us to remain indifferent.

The knowledge we have acquired regarding history and the real dimensions of humanity renders it even more agonizing. It was possible in certain epochs to believe that Christianity had been announced to the entire world, a relatively short time after Christ. On the other hand, an inadequate appreciation of mankind's past and especially the absence of a habit of considering it in all its profundity brought it about that people were less sensitive to these huge masses which for immensely long periods of time lived without contact with Christ. It would serve no purpose to observe that before Christ the Jewish people were the depositaries of the means of salvation; for the widening of our perspective has shown us how relatively few were the men who were in those days able to come into contact with the revelation made to Israel.

In short, the problem is not resolved even for those who, since the coming of Christ, have been able to know His Church exteriorly. Many reasons, in fact, among which must be numbered perhaps a more acute sense of values and of individual situations, aid us today in having an awareness that those to whom the Gospel was announced and who did not accept it as the message of salvation must not for all that, always be thought of as having lacked good will. I am not speaking merely of the deformities in the presentation of Christianity that may have prevented it from being seen in its true nature; nor of the errors of those who have linked it to contingent and sometimes positively unjust political and social forms.

But supposing that it had been presented without these deformities and free from these compromises, it remains that one does not make truth enter a spirit like one writes a sentence on a sheet of paper. Now then, as a result of prejudices anchored securely by early education, by prolonged formation, by the thinking habits of a whole environment, and not as a result of unfaithfulness to lights received, it may happen that certain spirits do not manage to represent Christianity to themselves just as it is; in reality they rebuff only the involuntarily erroneous interpretation they have put upon it. Just as there are invincible errors, it seems that in certain cases there are some practically invincible misunderstandings.

For all these reasons, it seems truly scandalous to exclude from salvation—the only thing that matters definitively—all those men of whom we can and must say that they lived visibly outside the Church. Otherwise it would be necessary to avow that the immense majority of mankind finds itself, willy nilly, not only off the normal path but actually off the path to salvation itself. Yet it is in this way that some understand Catholic doctrine on this subject. We have here precisely a typical example of those deformations, often involuntary, but too widespread, of the thought of the Church.

We certainly do not dream of putting in doubt nor of minimizing the importance or rather the necessity of the Church for salvation. But before explaining her role, and in order to be able to explain it correctly, it is necessary to recall other complementary statements. As Karl Adam says: "To understand this dogma 'No salvation outside the Church' in its true sense, one must see it in its origin and replace it in the ensemble of dogma. No Catholic truth forms a separate piece. Each has its place and its meaning in a whole system. It is only in the light of the whole that its true meaning can be found" (Le vrai visage du Catholicisme, p. 212). It is because this rule has been forgotten that insoluble problems often arise, that Christian truths are falsified while people think they are pushing them to their conclusions, that they are given a scandalizing appearance. But the statements we have recalled with regard to the necessity of

the Church do not abolish those of St. Paul in the Epistle
to the Romans, 2:9 ff.: "Tribulation and anguish shall
be visited upon the soul of every man who works evil;
of Jew first and then of Greek. But glory and honor
and peace shall be awarded to everyone who does good,
to Jew first and then to Greek. Because with God there
is no respect of persons. For whoever have sinned without the Law, will perish without the Law; and whoever
have sinned under the Law, will be judged by the Law.
For it is not they who hear the Law that are just in the
sight of God; but it is they who follow the Law that
will be justified. When the Gentiles who have no law
do by nature what the Law prescribes, these having no
law are a law unto themselves. They show the work of
the Law written in their hearts. Their conscience bears
witness to them, even when conflicting thoughts accuse
or defend them. This will take place on the day when,
according to my gospel, God will judge the hidden
secrets of men through Jesus Christ." *

Though everything in this passage is not clear, though
there are many difficulties as to details in its explanation,
one thing at least is clear, and that suffices for the moment. The pagans will not be judged according to a
Law they do not know, that is to say, according to the
written Law of the Jews, but according to the Law
which they possess in themselves—that is, based on what
they have been able to know about the Law of God by
means of their consciences. It is not said: according to
what they have explicitly recognized as the Law of God,
but according to this Law of God insofar as their consciences shall have made it known to them. We may interpret that they will be judged according to the light

* English rendition from Confraternity Edition of N.T.

they have possessed. They will not be condemned in the name of an obligation they have not been aware of—on the condition, of course, that this ignorance is not due to their own fault. This accuracy is important because a person can make himself capable of seeing, of better perceiving the full scope of a primary obligation, and we have the duty of doing all that is ours to do in order to arrive at that goal. It is necessary that everyone maintain a salutary restlessness about always remaining open to a possible increase of light, about not shutting oneself up even in a good conscience as though it were adequate without the desire of always enlightening it further. But, in short, no one will be judged according to a Law which, without its being his fault, has not been manifested to his conscience.

St. Paul is herein speaking directly only of the pagan and the Jew, and he cites only the Mosaic Law because in this portion of his Epistle to the Romans, it is the pagans and the Jews that are being discussed. Moreover let us note that the Law of Moses, with the knowledge of God and of morality which it brought, was prior to the Church, the providential institution for salvation. It is quite legitimate to make a transposition of this doctrine to what we are concerned with, after the appearance of the Church. I believe that the consequences that one is permitted to draw from the text of St. Paul are not at all exceeded when we add that among those who do not know the Church we have to include not only those who have never heard of her, but those who—always without any fault on their part—have not seen the obligation they had of entering in her, those whose lack of recognition of this obligation—which by right is incumbent on them—is not the result of unfaithfulness or negligence. It may be said that actually, the moral unanimity of the theologians admits that the concrete means of salvation is lacking to no soul of good will. Now for certain of these, for an immense number, the very knowledge of existence of the Church is or was impossible—for all those who lived or were still living, in nonevangelized regions. For the others, no definition of the Magisterium has ever proclaimed that only culpable obstacles could exist to recognition of the obligation of entering the Church.

On the other hand, this concrete possibility of salvation must not presuppose any miracle, because the law of miracles is rarity, and this involves innumerable cases. The words of St. Thomas stating that rather than leave one soul of good will in ignorance of the truths necessary for salvation, God would send him an angel, have been abused. The intention there is to affirm the impossibility of God's allowing a soul of good will to be lost for the lack of a means of salvation, much more than to specify the means God will employ to save it.

St. Thomas moreover has another doctrine which goes along in the exact same sense as what we wish to establish at this point. Explaining that no one can die with original sin to which only venial sin would have been added, he says that if man, as his reason unfolds, when placed in the position of orienting himself toward God or turning away from Him, turns to Him by an act of love, he is justified, freed from original sin; if on the other hand he turns away from God, he adds a mortal sin to original sin. Let us simply retain the idea that in the use of his reason, man has to take a stand with regard to God, and that this act will place him in the way of salvation or in that of perdition. That is a universal law which presupposes no miraculous intervention, and is not linked to any particular status of religious knowledge. Every man possesses concretely, therefore, the ability to place himself in the way of salvation.

That again is what is explicitly stated by Pius IX in his encyclical of August 10, 1863: "Men who are in invincible ignorance of our holy religion but who faithfully keep the natural law and its commandments, just as God has engraved them in all hearts, and who are disposed to obey God, who lead a morally irreproachable life, such men may, with the help of divine light and grace, obtain eternal life; for God, Who knows and penetrates the depths of all sentiments, movements, thoughts and interior states of souls, does not, in His infinite goodness and meekness, will that any of those who are not guilty of a voluntary fault perish eternally." And likewise, in an allocution of December 9, 1864: "We are far from wanting to place limits on the divine mercy which is infinite. We certainly do not want to scrutinize further the designs and secret judgments of God which are a profound abyss. . . . It is in fact a truth of Faith that no man may be saved outside of the Apostolic Roman Church, that she is the sole ark of salvation, and that those who do not take refuge in her are engulfed by the deluge. Nevertheless, it must be held as equally certain that those who are in ignorance of the true religion are not, if this ignorance is invincible, guilty of any fault in the eyes of God." But who would pretend to set the limits of this ignorance, with such a great variety of peoples and conditions? We have here, therefore, the very clear affirmation that no one can be condemned without a fault on his part, and that, given the complexity of the factors involved, a human eye cannot discern where there is culpability. That is a judgment only God can make.

III. *Attempt at a solution*

Out of this rather disparate ensemble of doctrines and documents, one thing stands out clearly. And that is that the traditional statement: "Outside of the Church there is no salvation" must not lead us to forget this other one: "No man, in whatever situation he finds himself, whether after or before Christ, will be condemned unless he has sinned against the light, unless he has some share of personal culpability in the religious ignorance in which he finds himself." And does that not satisfy all our legitimate susceptibilities? Reconciling these two statements may be difficult; but even if we do not succeed in doing so in a way that satisfies us, that will not serve us as a reason for abandoning one or the other of the two. For we hold both on the Faith of the Church. We must not therefore make their acceptance or rejection depend on the insufficiency of our vision.

As a consequence, everything here does not depend upon the value of the explanation we may be able to give. It may be useful all the same to look for such an explanation, because the necessity to which our spirit is thus placed—not of weakening two truths but of reconciling them to each other, of leading them into a superior unity, may be the means of casting greater light on one and the other, and of helping us by that very fact to a deeper understanding of our Faith.

First of all, it is very clear that all those who will be saved will be saved by the grace of Christ, no matter what may have been their religious status on earth. There is for mankind only one force which tears it from sin, and that is the grace of Christ. If men can be saved everywhere and in all times and environments, that proves simply that the grace of Christ is capable of acting everywhere. The Church has not accepted this doctrine of Saint Cyranus that: "Not a single drop of grace falls on the heathen." The ancient theologians, without sacrificing anything of the necessity of the Sacraments, used to say: "God has not tied His grace to the Sacraments," that is to say that He can, when He wills, when He judges it meet, communicate apart from the Sacraments the grace He normally gives by their means; which does not authorize us to impose on His goodness to remove ourselves from the economy established by Him when it is accessible to us. This grace leads all those men who receive it and who are faithful to it to union with Christ in eternity; there, then, they will be also united with those who will in turn be united to Christ. How could all those who are united to the same Christ not be united among themselves? How could they live with the life of the same Christ if they were to remain—not hostile, it is true, but separated from one another? All the saved, no matter what their status was on earth, will then be part of that spiritual community which is the Church of heaven.

Now she, as we have said, is not different from the Church of earth; she is the same Church in another state. In the first place, therefore, it is true—I am not saying that it is simply true—that there is no salvation outside the Church, because there is no salvation without entering this spiritual community which is the Church of heaven, the continuation, the transfiguration of the visible Church that shall have lived and fought, on this earth. There will be one only Church which, under the influence of Christ, will live of God. There will be no separate groups, there will be no different species of happiness.

There is only one way of escaping damnation: being joined to the unique Church of heaven; all of which, to be understood, demands that one renounce an individualistic (and if one is not careful, egotistical) conception of salvation. To be saved is not merely to be delivered from all forms of suffering, and to possess a solitary happiness; it is to recapture union with others, with all those who have not voluntarily cut themselves off, while recapturing union with God. It is to contribute in some fashion to the formation of the Body of the saved. There is then no obtaining of salvation except "in the form of a Church," in a spiritual community. And there will be no other community than that which will exist under Christ, and which is to be the definitive form of the one only Catholic Church. Thus, no salvation is possible without final integration into the Catholic Church: all of which demands that this idea of a Church, an idea that we have already fought against, be renounced—the idea of a Church that would be only a provisional organization, a simple means of salvation that the faithful would use provisionally, where they would be grouped for a time, but which would have no more "raison d'être" in the after-world, once the goal had been reached. Now, if it has been understood that, as we have just said, in salvation reunion with God and reunion with other men are inseparable, and that lacking one or the other, man would not be saved, that is to say torn from what causes his misery and misfortune, it will be understood that the Church must remain in heaven, though under different conditions. It is in her that the great gathering of the whole of saved mankind will take place. We therefore say it is toward this heavenly Church that grace has led and continues to lead souls who have not sinned against the light.

But there is something more. For all, the Church is more than the goal; she is also, in a sense that remains for us to define, the way. It is not only in the eternal Church that everyone will possess salvation; everyone already owes to the Church on earth the grace which is leading him there.

To understand this, it is important to form a correct idea of the plan of God and of its modes. We too easily imagine God dealing with each soul in particular, as if souls were isolated atoms, without any bond among them, and the means of salvation seem to us to be the object of a purely individual utilization, like a treasure placed by God at the disposition of souls of good will, from which each would come to draw for his own use. It is not thus that God was pleased to save men. Redemption is the replacing of mankind on the right path. God treats it as forming a real unit. That certain members withdraw from salvation by a personal refusal (and no one knows the number, not even whether it is large or small), does not alter the fact that in one sense it is mankind that is saved; it is mankind that has been given the ability to resume its march toward God. But how is this Redemption accomplished? How is the source of grace, tainted by sin, replaced in mankind? By the sacrifice of Christ of course. But the fruit of this sacrifice, the presence of grace, is linked in the plan of God to the existence of a Church, of a visible society which is the Catholic Church.

Though she only appeared at the end of a relatively

long time, she is at the beginning of the paths of God. She stands in the first rank among the divine intentions. And if her appearance was put off, it was not by an arbitrary measure and divine caprice; it is because time was needed to prepare for her (cf. the analogous problem, often treated of by the Fathers, of the preparation of Christ and the "delaying" of the Incarnation). Life and even the entire material world are for man, even though man himself appeared late, to the extent that it could be said that if there were never to have been a humanity neither would there ever have been a material world. Likewise, there would never have been any grace at work in the bosom of the human race, if there were not one day to be, if there were not today, the Church. The Church, as its end and condition, is therefore the explanation for the existence of grace. She it is in whom grace has taken root in mankind. The presence of grace in the world is bound up, by the Will of God, with the presence of the Church. This Will of God is by no means an arbitrary thing. We have already seen the equivalent of these statements, when we spoke of the visible Church as the Body of Christ. It is by the Church that Christ is present and active in mankind. Grace can act, it does act, outside the visible limits of the Church, but its presence and activity are nonetheless connected to the visible Church, from the moment that God linked up the salvation of the world with the constitution of a Church.

The sacrifice of Jesus Christ, willed by God in the economy of salvation, is destined to bear fruit through the Masses celebrated in the Church, Masses that are the sacramental renewal thereof—the two are inseparable. Without the Cross, the Mass would be only an empty ceremony; but by the same token, without the Mass, the Cross would be only a sort of sealed-up source. (Suppositions that are obviously impossible since God has willed both one and the other, of them.)

Also, without the sacrifice of the Church, offered by the Church, which is the Mass, there would not be any grace circulating in mankind. The graces which reach out to all the members of a redeemed mankind are due to the sacrifice offered by the Church. But in order to prove these considerations more conclusively, it is doubtless necessary to go a little deeper into them. The Church, as we have had occasion to say several times, is not something all completed, static; she is a growing reality whose goal is to spread out even to the very dimensions of mankind. This must be understood to mean not only in extent, geographically so to speak, but also qualitatively. She has to assimilate, in order to convert and transfigure it, whatever good is done in the human order. Nothing human is foreign to her. There is nothing she does not have to assume in order to consecrate it and offer it to the Lord, purified of all that might corrupt or lessen it. The Church exists before having accomplished this task. In her visible development she is subject to the law of time and growth, like all human institutions. (For though she is not merely a human institution, she is nevertheless truly a human institution too, just as Christ, who is not merely a man, is nonetheless truly a man.) At the outset, she is in possession of that divine force which is to permit her to assimilate and transform all things. But more than that, she cannot exist without tending to this end from the start, without beginning to act with a view to attaining it. Also, all those who, under the influence of grace, work toward the accomplishment of something good, something of value, something that represents a human value in the real sense of the word, in whatever situation they find themselves, are in reality working for the Church, even without knowing it. They are working for something that will in the end be taken back and consecrated by the Church, and that will have some kind of efficacity in bringing her to her goal.

There is then a link between their action and the Church. If they do not belong visibly to her, they are nevertheless not without some relationship to her. Not only that the grace which may exist in them could not be there without the existence of the Church, but also that their work prepares the Church's materials for her. We can understand then that they are able to benefit from the salvation brought to the world by Christ and carried out by the Church, and do so by reason of what they do for her without knowing it.

It is clear that all this holds true only for those men who are visibly outside the Church through no fault of their own. For those who have become aware of their obligation to belong to the Church, or those who have not heard this call because they were not willing to place themselves in the conditions that would have allowed them to hear it, those who, being called to do more, deliberately chose to be content with less; all of them have it charged against their account, as it were, that they refuse; it is their resistance that describes them. Having rejected the means of salvation, they can no longer benefit from it, were it even by secret paths.

Quite different is the position of those who, even amidst errors and guiltless gropings, have followed as best they could the inspirations of the nameless grace which made them develop in themselves whatever they found around them that was valuable and fruitful. Since the Church is enriched by a civilization she penetrates, since the Christian Body profits from everything good that accumulates among errors and inadequacies, is it not normal for those who without having sinned against the light, have contributed even from afar in constituting and enriching her, to receive their share of the salvation brought by this Church for which they have labored? And is it not right in that case to say that they are saved by the virtue of this Church, since in the final analysis what effects their salvation is that they have worked for her without knowing it, to the best of their ability? If every sincere effort toward justice and charity, even if made beyond the visible boundaries of the Church, is capable of some day profiting the visible body of Christians, because it can reveal to them new forms of justice and charity they will have to promote, is it not normal again that those who have tried to the best of their ability, without turning a deaf ear to the mysterious call they were receiving therefrom, should benefit from the salvation brought by the Church?

Therefore, not only is no one ever saved except by a grace which is bound up with the existence of the Church, but too, no one is ever saved except with relation to this unique Church because without knowing it, one lives by her and lives for her as best he can. Of all those who have these salutary dispositions it can be said that they are already in the Church "by desire." In fact, if they have this implicit will to follow the light of grace and to respond to all its demands, in the event that they were to realize the necessity of entering the Church, they would respond to it immediately. They would not then have to make a new decision to place an act changing their direction; they would only have to carry forward the movement which already animated them. If they were to refuse it, which is always a possibility, then it is that they would be revoking their prior wish and would leave the state of grace which was theirs on the path of salvation. Whether they succeed in meeting the Church that up to then they had not known, or whether they learned to comprehend her true role in the designs of God, they will spontaneously realize that their place is there.

That is why this doctrine cannot encourage any contempt for the visible Church nor engender a lessened esteem for membership in the Church among those who are already visibly her members. No one has the right to say: since a person can be saved without belonging visibly to the Church, why should there be an absolute obligation of entering her or of remaining in her? For, a person is saved without being so visibly only because he is so disposed as to be visibly (a member) if the necessity for it were perceived, that is if he became aware of the Divine Plan and of the commandment which ensues. If those who are already in the Church or who have recognized the need for entering her were to decide to put themselves in the external situation of those of whom we are speaking, they would not really have the same inward dispositions. That is what Cardinal Deschamps gave to understand in a few words: one day he said in answer to a lady who was pursuing precisely the idea that one can be saved without belonging visibly to the Church: "Madam, that is true, but it no longer concerns you."

In recent enough times, it was the custom to speak of

those who are in this way visibly outside the Church but who nevertheless inwardly belong to her, since they are saved through her, as belonging to the "soul of the Church," by contrast to the people who are visibly in her and of whom it was said that they belonged to her Body. This manner of speaking was not retained by the Vatican Council. It is generally abandoned today. People rightly prefer to say that they belong invisibly to the Body of the Church, or to the Body of Christ which is the Church (*Corpus Christi quod est Ecclesia*). That is because the Church is indeed a body, and one must belong to this body to be saved. The expression "soul of the Church" can be understood in a good sense, but it is less theological, and was not traditional. Moreover, it could lend favor to the idea of an invisible Church which would be more truly the Church than is the visible Church.

On the other hand, everything we have said shows that there is a link, a real relationship between these non-believers and the visible reality, the visible activity of the Church, although this relationship, by hypothesis, is not known to them and though they do not belong to the Church by the normal visible marks, Baptism and the profession of Faith.

11

The Church and the Temporal Order

Up to now we have considered the Church in herself, in her own constitution and in her religious activity; or rather—since all her activity is religious—we have considered her only where her activity is exercised on exclusively religious terrain. We are going to see today how she intervenes, for religious reasons, on terrain that is not exclusively religious. This is the question ordinarily treated under the name of the relations between Church and State. I prefer to speak, in a more general fashion, of the relation between the Church and the temporal order, because the problem of the Church and the State is in reality but one of the cases—one of the most important, it is true, and without a doubt the most delicate—of intervention of the Church in the temporal order.

In pagan society, the city and religion are closely united. One may say that they are but one. The City has a religious character, and religion has a political character. Everyone belongs *de jure* to the cult of his City; and too, irreligion is a crime punished by law. There is no place for the existence of a distinct Church; the city itself regulates Worship. (We are obviously just outlining; thus, the identity between clergy and civil magistrates is not always absolute; thus too, at certain epochs, for example in the Hellenistic Age, certain forms of worship are seen to develop that, up to a certain point, free themselves from political frameworks). Among the Jewish people, too, for altogether different reasons, there is no distinction between the temporal and the religious. For it is a people in the carnal sense of the word that God first of all chose and in whose bosom was prepared the Coming of the Messias. But the fusion here was made in the inverse sense: it was religion, under varying forms, that more or less absorbed politics.

Our Lord affirms the transcendant nature of religion which must not be put to the service of human ends, and He founded the Church which has charge of religious life. But He does not for all that deny the legitimacy of the temporal order. His words presuppose that there is an order of things in which "Caesar," that is the human authority, has the right to command and be obeyed. There is a human political order, a non-theocratic State. But Caesar is not God, and everything in man does not depend on him.

From that we must not conclude to the separation, pure and simple, of the two domains, that of Caesar and that of God. It would be a misconception of the whole teaching of Christ regarding God to imagine that Caesar can be placed in juxtaposition to Him. If there is a distinction between the two orders, there is also a certain relationship of subordination of one to the other. God is not on the same level as Caesar. The religious order and the temporal order cannot therefore be simply coordinated, as if it were a question of two similar and sufficiently distinct domains, wherein are exercised two independent authorities. It is therefore necessary to set down precisely the *sui generis* relationship between the religious order and the temporal order—that order wherein Caesar, that is, the State, is of course not everything, but does occupy a central position.

Mankind is created for a supernatural end, the possession of God in love. This end cannot be known, nor the way leading thereto, nor can one enter upon this way effectively, without a revelation from God and the gift of His grace. This revelation is not given directly to each individual, and this gift of grace is normally linked to determinate external means (the Sacraments). Revelation is made by Jesus Christ, Eternal Word of God, Who did not confide it to a book, but to a Church, to which He also gave these Sacraments. In short, as we have seen, Christ founded a Church in which He lives, through which He rules our whole supernatural life. That is the "raison d'être" of the Church and her proper function, which is wholly in the religious order.

But man's supernatural calling does not tear him away from his natural life. He is not only pressed unceasingly by the need for providing for the immediate necessities of life, but also capable of a continuing search for beauty and truth, of creating social relationships which go beyond the demands of material usefulness, in short, of seeking out the goods of culture and of creating civilization. Now all of this enters into the divine plan. God

has created a world which is, from the natural and also
the supernatural point of view, incomplete, and which
has possibilities of developments in all spheres of the
body and of the spirit. Now on the natural level, mankind develops through its own efforts, thanks to its own
labors. There are then two distinct orders which we
may call the temporal and the religious order; the man
and the Christian, natural life and supernatural life do
not overlap sufficiently. Still, it is the same being that
has to be concerned with the temporal and live religi-
ously, it is the same being that is at once man and Christian. It is not possible to make a complete cleavage between the two. There is a perpetual interaction of one
upon the other. It is in this way that the organization of
the temporal order can make easier or on the contrary
more difficult for the average run of mankind, the
practice of what is required in the light of the supernatural end.

Even more, Christianity teaches firmly that the last
end of man does not reside in organizing an order which
would reach its completion in this world. But with
equal firmness it also teaches that man must not tend
to the possession of God while scorning the natural development of mankind in time, so as to concern himself only with his individual perfection (in that way he
could but miss out on it) or of the internal perfecting
of others. Of course, there are, if we may say it, spe-
cializations. But the very ones who give themselves exclusively to a certain task—and it is good, it is necessary
that there be some of those—must not become interested
in it as though all human development, outside of the
strictly religious plane, had no value from God's point
of view, as though it were something totally indifferent

and perhaps even harmful. There would be in that a serious deviation, a sort of pseudo-mysticism that does not conform to the Christian concept. According to the latter, mankind must tend to God, Whom it will reach only beyond the present life, and that obliges it always to raise itself above the purely temporal level and to refuse to rejoice in human values as an unsurpassable absolute.

But in order to attain its end, it must nonetheless pursue its natural development in all domains; only it has to be an ordered, hierarchical development, brought into harmony with the seeking of the last end in an afterlife. Leaving men in ignorance, in lack of culture, in disorder or in an inhuman order, enslaved to the forces of matter, is not compatible with this enlightened pursuit of the transcendent end. It may be done in very good faith, but it is nonetheless a mistake. The paradox of man understood in a Christian sense is, therefore, as follows: it is a matter of pursuing, in the temporal and in part through the temporal, an end which will only be reached beyond the temporal; of pursuing in and through work on oneself, on others, on the world, an end which will not be attained by work but rather thanks to an intervention from on high, an end that nevertheless cannot be obtained if this work is scorned.

We will try to indicate the points of contact which derive from this paradoxical situation, and we will see how they justify an intervention by the Church that resounds even in the temporal order, though her proper function is not to organize nor to rule this temporal order, but to guide the religious life of men.

First of all, it is necessary to preserve Christian life from the danger of absorption in the purely human life, which would cause the very condition of all religious life to disappear, or what amounts to the same thing— would cause religious life to be conceived as destined simply to provide a more potent dynamism, indispensable in the pursuit of the broadest and most elevated ends. The Church therefore intervenes to call to mind that, although it is legitimate and praiseworthy to work for the conquest of the world, as well as for giving value to all human wealth, nevertheless mankind is not destined to find here below its completion nor its balance. It will not find these except in an after-life, by the achievement of a state that cannot be the object of conquest but only a gift. The Church will also recall to man that he is not simply an incomplete being in an incomplete world (from the natural point of view), but that he is a sinful creature who must incessantly purify himself and defend himself against the tendencies which are constantly dragging him down. Nor is this without practical consequences; the entirety of Christian asceticism in temporal activity derives from it, along with the attitude of prudence, with the mastery of self in the handling of what is permissible. The Church does not forbid us this temporal activity; quite the opposite. Nor does she teach us the techniques that we must employ. But she does remind us that we must not give ourselves to it as if we were entirely pure beings, without any deviated tendencies. Without destroying any enthusiasm in us, she protects us from intoxication. All of this refers to a general atmosphere, the conditions under which man's activity operates; but it still does not constitute the source of the Church's interventions on precise points, even when her teachings or her warnings in some way touch upon our temporal activity.

What will provoke and serve as the basis for a more direct intervention is the *question of sin*. Our temporal activity in all the domains in which it is exercised, (family life, economic life, political and social life, intellectual life), is a free activity in which we choose (at least in a certain measure) the ends we propose for ourselves and the means for attaining them. It thereby belongs in the sphere of moral life. Now the Church is the guardian of morality by virtue of her religious function. That is because morality is essentially the Law of God governing the free activity of man. And one cannot progress toward the possession of God by disobeying Him; every disobedience of God is a sin, which compromises the supernatural life and which, when it is grave, goes so far as to destroy the state of grace. Though there are, obviously, social activities of all sorts that are of a purely temporal order and not properly religious, these activities, where they do touch upon moral life, often have repercussions in the religious life of the one who carries them out, and for this reason it becomes clear that one cannot make an absolute separation between the temporal and the religious orders.

Now the Church is the mistress of religious life; she it is who is charged with teaching us and prescribing to us in the name of Christ what is necessary, for forbidding us what is opposed to the preservation of this life, that is, with showing us what is sinful and reminding us of the prohibition of sin in all our activities whatever they may be. Thus, she will find herself forced to forbid us certain actions which, objectively, are in the temporal order. Certain ways of leading conjugal or family life, certain practices in economic relationships, certain aesthetic concepts, etc.; for example, theft, adultery, divorce, sterilization, abortion, etc., are actions which, while being situated in the order of temporal activity, fall under the spiritual jurisdiction of the Church because, as sins, they destroy supernatural life.

Another reason that might in certain cases motivate the intervention of the Church is in the domain of natural knowledge. In this domain, truth depends on the intellect. The Church, charged with religious truth, does not have the mission of teaching it. When the intelligence errs, that is not a sufficient reason for the Church to undertake to put it on the right track again. She has not received any lights for that. But it can happen that the human intellect, mistaken as to its own limitations, may want to solve a question which depends on Faith, or even say that all truth depends on it alone and consequently throw the whole domain of faith into illusions. Then the Church is in her province; she will have both the power and the duty to intervene. She knows that she holds the treasure of the revealed truth of God, which she has the mission of transmitting. She cannot allow it to be lessened, corrupted, nor treated as an illusion. She will say therefore that the human intellect is going beyond its proper boundaries in denying a domain which is above it, or in wishing to penetrate it. In intervening in this way, you see that she does so not because she has to straighten out the intellect each time it makes a mistake, but because she has her own domain to defend. In no way then is she stepping out of her religious function.

Another analogous case where again the Church can and must intervene. Certain "natural" truths, that is, truths accessible to the efforts of the intellect without the help of Faith, happen to be conditions of the truth of teachings in the supernatural order. Such, for example, are the reality of the spiritual soul, or the historical existence of Jesus Christ. If someone denies them, the Church steps in once again to protect the truths with which she is charged. It must be noted that then she is not concerned with discussing, with refuting the arguments that have been used to attack these natural truths; she leaves this concern to individual initiative. She simply says: such a statement cannot be true because it destroys the truth of which I am the depositary and that I hold from God. There again, she makes no invasion into a foreign domain. Thus there is, in the temporal order of practical or intellectual activities, a whole non-Christian way of acting to proscribe. It is insofar as she is charged with insuring the Christian life that the Church indicates what this non-Christian conduct consists of and in its place promulgates prohibitions.

Up to now, we have considered the prohibitions of the Church by reason of the possibility of a conflict when temporal or natural activity harms the religious order. There are in the world all sorts of situations which, given what man is, constitute for him conditions that are favorable or unfavorable to his religious life, that is, to his progress toward God. Certainly when one is decided to go as far as martyrdom, nothing prevents living in a Christian manner. Among the perfect, every obstacle turns into a means. But that presupposes a high degree of religious life, and though one must want to lead all men to such heights, it is not there that one has to begin. Too great obstacles would not habitually be overcome by average men even if sincerely Christian and mindful of the moral law. It is this view of elementary wisdom in one of its chief applications that

Leo XIII recalls in the Encyclical "Rerum Novarum": a certain well-being is the normal condition for the aggregate of men, to practice virtue. Conversely, too great wealth is a great danger; it is difficult for the rich to be saved. Likewise, the absence of sanctions in a regime that is too easy, or on the contrary, too harsh an authority in the State, in professional life, in the family, lead to many condemnable practices. There again you see, it is a question of living conditions of the temporal order, not the religious order. It is indeed a matter of the redistribution of wealth, of the organization of society, of civil government, etc. . . . all of them things which are not in themselves religious, but which entail all sorts of religious consequences, because they favor either sin or virtue. The Christian has the duty therefore of creating, in the measure his influence permits him to, a temporal situation that favors the observation of the moral law and of religious life. It is up to the Church to remind him of it, by recalling to him that the whole human order must help the supernatural life, since the final purpose of creation is the supernatural end of mankind. It is up to the Church who knows what this end is that is given to man, and who knows also what is the real situation of this man, in what and how he is attacked by sin, to say also what in general are the conditions in which the human order will play its part, and to determine some of its essential features. Again, therefore, it is up to her by that very fact to denounce situations in which these conditions are too greatly misunderstood.

But whereas the Church in this way recalls the necessity of working to realize these conditions, she does not for all that trace out the detailed plan of an ideal City, and she does not, moreover, say what are the concrete means to take to build it, given the actual circumstances in which people find themselves (for example in a certain stage of development of science and industrial techniques). She does not have any special lights on that. She only touches on these problems insofar as they themselves touch on what concerns her divine mission. But in order to solve them in a way that will satisfy her, it behooves all Christians to study them at once in her spirit and also with all the resources of their human abilities; it is important that they seek with ardor and practical sense what, in given circumstances, are the organizations of a political, economic or social nature that will best lead to this end: to furnish to the aggregate of men those conditions favorable to a truly human life, itself a condition of the supernatural life.

But in addition to this there is a more intimate relationship between the temporal and supernatural orders, one which flows from the unity of God's plan. And this new relationship justifies another type of intervention on the part of the Church. The future possession of God will be the blossoming of the grace that is given to us already here below not only as a promise or a pledge, but as an advance deposit. Therefore, our accomplishments in this world are somehow to be, if we are faithful to grace, the rough draft of what the celestial City will be. For inner dispositions are real only to the extent that they tend to be translated into our actions. The grace that dwells in a Christian tends to inspire his whole life; it wants to be the source of all his activity, it tolerates nothing in his conduct that might be opposed to it.

Now this grace, in its fullest flowering, is the possession

of God by charity; it is indissolubly the love of God and of neighbor. That is by way of saying that the Christian, if he is faithful to its inspiration, will want to make the earthly city into the least imperfect possible image of the heavenly City. He is in a position to fulfill this ideal, of course, only in his individual attitude, and he cannot answer for the conduct of someone else. But he will seek to carry out in all things the conditions of this mutual charity in his public life as well as in the relationships of his private life. For charity should dominate the life of the entire world, should inspire it in its very structures. Therefore it is not only with an eye to fostering religious life in the narrow sense of the word that one must seek to make injustice, violence, etc., disappear, but it is because these evils are contrary to the expression of Charity; in other words because they are in themselves evil things.

This must not be taken in a Utopian sense—that would compromise the small success it is permissible to expect from it. A considerable share of constraint will always be necessary in the groundwork of social life. But this very constraint can be variously inspired, variously oriented; it should be by Charity. Certainly we know only too well that the earth will never be perfect; we know that the greatest successes, no matter how varied, always leave society exposed to relapses. But that does not change the fact that the will to progress, the effort toward better things is always demanded of us.

The same truth could be presented by starting with the ideal of unity, or better of community, that Our Lord requires of His disciples. This community finds its crowning only in participation in the same Church, and even within this Church it will be perfect only in heaven. That is what we have seen in preceding lessons. But the Church would not think of approving of those Christians who would deliberately limit their charity to the order of "ecclesiastical" relationships. A life of community must tend to surpass the framework of the strictly religious life. All of these constitutions, all of these social organizations should foster it insofar as possible. That does not at all mean that religious and civil society must tend to be confused. Nor does that mean that all hierarchy and all distinction would have to be suppressed. Nothing is less "one" than a mob. There are moreover several possible types of societies, one and all more or less capable of being Christianized. But the Christian does not give an absolute and definitive value to any particular temporal order. He is always ready to place it again in question under conditions required by prudence, certainly not out of anarchy or a morbid need for change, but when circumstances make it possible, to better adapt it to its end which is to allow and promote partially in its own way community relationships among men.

What will the intervention of the Church be like on this terrain? It will consist in recalling in its entire positive extent, that law of Charity which must dominate all our activity. In so doing, she will remind us of the profound meaning of the entire temporal order, and the orientation we have to give it. As for what is concretely possible to accomplish, it is up to the initiative of the Christian, each in his own sphere, to figure out and to attempt. The measure cannot always be the same. In a civilization where Christian spirit has already penetrated somewhat, it is necessary to have a better understanding of the need to tend toward a real unity. What seems allowable or final in a given century may afterwards seem to be no longer tolerable. Here the Church acts less by direction than by a sort of enveloping influence, and without quitting the religious terrain she acts efficaciously upon the temporal by instigating many transformations.

Now we will consider, in a few words, the particular problem posed by the State. The State, or the political power, is necessary to insure temporal good order and the development of mankind, so that the Church admits not only its legitimacy but its absolute necessity. Each individual therefore has the obligation of recognizing the State, and consequently of obeying it when it performs its function properly. Since, on the other hand, there is a society endowed also with authority, the Church, that is charged with revealing to man his transcendental end and to lead him to it, it follows that the Christian, that is, the man who recognizes the authority of the Church, is subject at once to a double power: a political power and a religious power—or as it is often said, a "temporal" and a "spiritual" one. The State does not set the conditions of the total development of man; it only sets the conditions of the temporal order.

Though in a sense it may be said of it as of every human thing that it has a supernatural end because in the long run everything must converge toward the supernatural end, nevertheless it has only to occupy itself with certain temporal conditions for this end (which does not mean, as the tendency sometimes is to interpret it, that it is competent only on the material level). On her side, the Church has no temporal jurisdiction. That is not inferiority on her part; it is just that she is kept for a higher task. The State, then, receives its power from God, not from the Church. It is not her delegate, her executive agent. It is sovereign in its order. The Church attests to the existence or non-existence of the political power; she does not confer it. But as interpreter of the Natural Law, she fixes limits for it and determines the domain that is its own. For she is the one who knows the total order, since she knows the last end and can thus enlighten each of those who more or less directly work therein in their own place, in the overall plan. Here when we say "the Church," we mean her doctrine, her authentic teaching; because it is of course possible that the pretentions of a particular man of the Church may be exaggerated and History furnishes us examples of that.

It comes about that the Church reminds the State—she already does so by her very existence—that it has no hold on the total man. The State must not misconceive the relative and subordinate nature of the order it represents—vast and important as this order may be. *A fortiori* must it not reverse the roles and consider the Church, her doctrine, her influence, as means it can utilize in its own way to attain its own ends. It is always a temptation for the State, when it does not persecute the Church, to use her as an auxiliary and to measure the favors it grants her by the direct services it expects from her. The Church is constantly obliged to react against this desire to enslave her. She is, in particular, charged with the religious and moral education of her members because she is capable of discerning these values in all domains; she cannot consent to let them be dictated to her. Nor can she allow herself to be pushed back into the realm of "private life"; she gives out the principles of social and civic morality as well as those of individual morality.

By virtue of her spiritual jurisdiction in the order of morality, the Church can pronounce on certain actions of the State. She does not judge them from a technical point of view, that is to say, insofar as they are proper means for attaining a definite temporal end, but solely from a moral point of view, when moral principles are in play. She is not qualified to know whether this certain tax system, for example, is suitable for furnishing the State with the resources it needs; or whether such and such a professional organization must contribute to insure the efficient operation of commerce or industry. But she can judge that a certain measure is unjust, that it violates a law of conscience.

It is therefore only inasmuch as they may be sins that actions relating to the temporal organization fall within the jurisdiction of the Church. She then condemns them as contrary to morality and forbids her faithful to carry them out (that is, forbids the one who governs to prescribe them, the one who is governed to execute them). This prohibition is not directed to the governor or the governed as such, after the manner of a political constitution, a civil law or a governmental act; it is directed to his conscience. It is not an act of political authority on the part of the Church, but of a moral command. Let us not even say that the political authority is reached thereby because it is linked to the moral; let us merely say, in a more precise and restrained way, that the political is reached through the moral. It is always solely from the moral and religious angle that the Church approaches the question. It is not she who forges a link between the moral and the temporal; they are necessarily linked in the degree that temporal actions, being human and free acts, are subject to the moral law.

The Church then does not take away, even partially, the power of those who use it wrongly. Whatever may have been the case in certain actions of the past, which are explained by the historical situation, and the evolution of public law, she does not recognize that power in herself today. She only says, when the occasion forces her to it, that where authority commands evil, one has no right to obey, because "it is better to obey God than men." She is moreover more inclined in these matters to preach moderation than intransigence. Christians always have the right, as citizens, of seeking to change an unjust or tyrannical power by methods in conformity with morality; but as long as they have not arrived at that point they owe it obedience in everything that is not contrary to the law of God.

The Church, which makes it an obligation for her faithful to work to change unjust and persecutory laws, does not oblige them to change the government or regime which authors them. You see then how the Church, while condemning in the name of morality certain abuses of power and while claiming the right to do so, does not arrogate to herself any authority over the power itself, any jurisdiction of a political nature over the State.

The power of the Church thus defined is often called nowadays the *indirect power*. This concept of it is therefore opposed to the concept of a direct power of the Church over the temporal which would consist in seeing the State as a sort of delegate of the Church for temporal affairs. This expression "indirect power" is a good one itself. Nevertheless it risks being equivocal because it has served to define theories that were slightly different. "Directive power" has also been proposed. That expression is not well-chosen because in the cases we have just considered, the Church gives real orders (or rather she issues true prohibitions), based on the need for spiritual sanctions, and not simply "directives." The expression "directive power" therefore risks confusing the exercise of the power of intervening with full authority in the name of morality, with the use of the right equally possessed by the Church of giving directives or counsels in certain circumstances without fully engaging all her authority.

There are indeed cases where the adoption of such a definite attitude in a temporal matter is liable to entail serious repercussions on the spiritual interests the Church has to guard. If neither of the attitudes between which a choice is to be made constitutes a sin, the Church will not give orders properly so called. She can nevertheless demand that her faithful, especially a certain category of the faithful, adopt the attitude she judges the most proper for safeguarding the spiritual interests involved. Those are directives, whose form moreover can be more or less urgent, and which do not bind by virtue of obedience but rather by virtue of prudence, since one can and must presume that they are not given lightly and since no one has the right seriously to compromise spiritual interests. Therefore, for the one who receives the directive, there is a duty, since prudence is not a facultative virtue and its exercise can be obligatory. However if, on the other hand, one has serious reasons for thinking that the conduct which is advised against does not present the feared inconveniences, but that on the contrary there would be a real danger to spiritual interests in following the directive, the obligation ceases. Of course one must be competent to make this judgment. Someone may have reasons, then, that make it not imprudent to depart from a directive that has been received; but the reasons will have to be all the more serious as the directive comes from higher up.

As an example, we may cite here the question of the "Rallying." In 1892, Leo XIII asked French Catholics to rally to the republican form of government of their country. He felt that a prolonged opposition on their part to the plans of the political regime would be harmful to the position of Catholicism in France. As a matter of fact, the government gave as a reason for the persecution begun against the Church, the bond which existed between her and the political parties of the constitutional opposition. Judging it to be in the Church's interest to remove all appearances of cogency in that reason, Leo XIII was asking Catholics, not to renounce their personal preferences, but to cease such opposition, even by legitimate methods, so as to be better able to defend religion. Constitutional opposition carried on by upright methods is not a sin; there was not, then, in that, any application on the Church's part of her power to condemn a political persuasion insofar as it is contrary to the moral law. But Leo XIII thought that the sacrifice he was asking of part of the French Catholics would have a happy result for the Church. As long therefore as his directive was in effect, it obliged in the name of prudence.

Whenever Churchmen try, in the name of their religious authority, to exercise control, to exert any kind of influence that goes beyond the limits recognized by the Christian doctrine on the intervention of the Church in temporal matters, over political affairs, there is what is called *clericalism*. But the name clericalism must not be given to every Church decision, based on what we have just considered, regarding a political question.

12

The Church and the Missions

I am tempted to adopt instead as a title: The Church and the Mission, to underline properly that there is question of a fundamental activity of the Church of which "the missions" are applications. Indeed, they are not undertakings of a more or less peripheral nature with no link among them. Nevertheless, I will keep to the consecrated terminology, recalling at the outset, however, that what we have to study is the sense and scope of missionary activity. What we must see is what this activity reveals to us about the nature of the Church, how it makes us understand more profoundly this Church by which we live. In inviting you today, therefore, to reflect on this missionary activity, I am inviting you not only to think of others, of all those who have not yet received the preaching of the Gospel; I would especially want to make you realize what you yourselves have to be in order to live fully of the life of the Church, instead of being simply installed in the Church. Naturally, the fact of thinking about the missions leads us to think of others. But these two kinds of thinking are not opposed to one another; what is even better, they are not basically different, for, as we are going to see, a Christian would not be able to understand himself by looking only at himself. He understands himself only in his relationship to others, by his relationship to others . . . to all others.

If missionary activity, taken in all its extent and force, is really an essential activity of the Church, then it will only be understood as a manifestation of the very being of the Church; that is, it will have to be related to the fundamental traits of the constitution of the Church—taking "constitution" here not in the juridical sense, but rather in a sense that could be called biological, since missionary activity expresses the living reality of the Church, the reality of the Church considered as a living entity.

I. *Meaning and Scope of Missionary Activity*

The Church, writes Father Pierre Charles, is today like a child who lacks no organ, but must still quadruple, quintuple its height and weight. "This law of growth, written into the body of a child, secret and active in the grain of mustard seed, is likewise imperious in the body of the Church, and the Sovereign Pontiffs who insistently remind us of that are but giving a voice to the silent clamor of the Church which has to grow" (*La Prière Apostolique*—Xaveriana). There is then a law of growth in the Church—a law not in the simple sense of an external command she might have received, but in the sense of an internal principle, an organic effort. The Church has within herself the power of assimilating and of transforming the entirety of mankind, even to its innermost fibers, and she must and wants to deploy this power completely.

We are not saying that this growth has to be continuous, as is that of the human body which grows unto its full stature. Christians do not know in advance what will be the success of their efforts either in extent or in depth. It is possible that the Church know periods of stagnation, even of regression, either from the point of view of numbers of faithful, or from the point of view of the fervor of the Christian nucleus. She has already known some. In return, she will not know any period of old age wherein the powers go into a fatal decline and where the organism marches irremediably on toward death. The life that animates the Church renders her always capable of new external expansion and of an incessant interior renewal. In this sense the Church is ever young, ever capable of growth. For her the fatal moment never comes when she could do no more than hang on, awaiting the decline. And no matter what vicissitudes she may have to pass through, the will to grow without cease unto the limits of humanity remains always in her.

1. This will to grow that we have wished to stress from the start as a characteristic of the Church must not be conceived as a will-to-live that could easily become a will-to-impose. It is not a kind of imperialism. It is the will to communicate the wealth she possesses. For, to the Church, to be more is not to dominate more, not to have a higher place among institutions that matter: it means enriching more beings, and enriching them more profoundly. It cannot be otherwise, because what the Church possesses, in the last analysis, is charity, par-

ticipation in the life of the Trinity. Now, a person cannot possess charity without wanting to communicate it
universally. That is the reason why the Church, spontaneously so to speak, tries to reach a specific human
group set apart either by its situation in the world, or by
its ethnic configuration, or by its civilization, each time
that one is revealed to her. To do so she does not wait to
have finished her task elsewhere. She will never allow
this to be said: we cannot cope with the work where we
are already set up; it is no time to go and increase our
work by undertaking the evangelization of a new people, in conditions that in the beginning are perforce very
difficult. No, the Christian spirit understands that it is
wise, in this sense, to disperse, and that on the other
hand, it would be nonsense to limit oneself in order to
concentrate. The Church thereby affirms in action her
will to communicate what she possesses to all mankind.
It is an effective way for her to show that she is not
limited to any one entourage, to any one people, to any
definite race, but that her charity is truly universal, that
is, that she possesses true charity, the kind that extends
to all without distinction.

    Also, she will send out missionaries—and she always
finds some—even to peoples on the decline, to those
which, humanly speaking, are finished, those which are
on the way to disappearing, as well as to those which
have the future before them and seem to bear in themselves man's future. There is a profuseness in that, a lack
of reckoning that human wisdom does not comprehend.
But since charity exists only if it wishes to spread itself,
since she herself is this effort at universal giving, the
Church exists truly only if she is universally missionary.
She does not start by being fulfilled, being settled in one

point of the globe, and wish to spread elsewhere only afterwards; from the very first instant, her existence implies the will to spread everywhere, "even to the ends of the earth." If she did not want to be everywhere, if she did not try to do so, she would be nowhere.

Often, the question of the necessity of the missions is posed by starting from the vantage point of the infidels who are to be evangelized, by considering the needs of the pagan masses. This is legitimate and indispensable. But the problem must also be treated as a function, we might say, of the Christian masses. We may ask ourselves if the missions are useful to or necessary for the pagans; it should perhaps be shown that they are necessary for Christians. We will understand this if we understand on the one hand that Christianity lived is the life of Charity, and on the other hand, that the life of Charity does not exist without a tendency to be communicated.

The sentiments of the Church, sentiments that every Christian has to make his own, could be expressed by this word of St. Paul: "*Woe to me if I preach not the Gospel.*" (Paul has just explained why he is renouncing, for his own part, the advantages that an apostle can normally expect from those he is evangelizing). The impulse comes from within. Thus it is with the missionary drive of the Church, with the missionary desire of the Christian.

2. Here then is the first reason for the Church's effort to expand. Here is how the Church is drawn to every new form of humanity that is revealed to her, to manifest her universality. There is another reason, another way of looking at things. When the Church goes forth to a people that has not as yet received the Faith, she is going forth to meet a grace of God. In fact, grace is at

work in every human group, in each man; it operates in each case toward an original effect, but an effect which can end up only in the Church and by her. Thus she is not simply going toward a void to fill it up. She is drawn there by a call from God. Those to whom she goes have no awareness of this call. She, however, hears it, because she is more clairvoyant regarding man than man himself; she knows him in his innermost reality more profoundly than he knows himself. She sees him in his position before God and in God's designs for him. Now in every people, despite innumerable failings, and innumerable refusals, despite all the opacity, too, that individuals cannot do away with all at once, the grace of God pursues this providential preparation whose term must be the adhering of this people to the Church, bringing with it its original features and its own wealth. There, too, is what makes for the imperious and sacred character of missionary activity (though it must always be exercised in patience): it is concerned with "rescuing" and "completing" a divine grace.

In the Epistle to the Romans, St. Paul speaks of natural creation which groans in expectation of the redemption of the sons of God; he shows it hoping to be delivered from the slavery to which it is subjected by man's sin. It seems to me that one could without temerity employ this image with regard to the peoples who await the Faith. Through the virtue of the grace already working in them, they groan, not in despair, but in expectation of the liberation the Church is to bring them; liberation from all chains, from all the inner deformations that sin merits for them, so that their spiritual being might finally blossom out in the light of Christ. The benefit of this deliverance therefore will not be theirs

alone; the whole Body of Christ into which they have
entered will benefit from it, for they will help her to
exploit in a new way the treasure which she has received from God and whose fecundity is unlimited.
Therein also the missions appear as the actualizing of the
catholicity of the Church—not only by giving her more
members, or even qualitatively varied members, but by
causing all the variety of the Divine Gift to burst forth
in the light of day.

We have already touched upon this question in speaking of catholicity. A while ago we were saying that we
must not be considered like those who possess and afterwards want to give, but rather that we possess only in
the very will to spread what we receive by grace. Now,
considering the matter from another aspect, we add that
we are not to be considered, either, as giving to others
who would have but to receive, but as giving to others
from whom we also are to receive, and perhaps much
more than we shall have given. Love among us is not
authentic if we do not desire to receive in turn, for the
"edification" of the Church, from those to whom we
give today. Christians who bring Faith to those who do
not as yet have it, are preparing to be someday their
debtors. An interchange is being set up. Missionary activity completes a circuit of grace.

I did not show you one of the "raisons d'être" of the
missions while speaking of the salvation of the infidels.
That would have been to broach from an individual
standpoint in a book on the Church a matter that is
essentially a matter of the Church. Thus we would have
let slide the most important aspects which alone can
afford a solution. And even the most apt of observations

would not have kept us from falling into multiple difficulties.

Are we to say, as has often been said, that the missions are necessary in order to bring salvation to individuals who cannot be saved as long as they are visibly outside the Church? But then we run up against the truth that salvation is not impossible for some men who do not belong visibly to the Church. We have shown how the two aspects of the truth are reconciled. I know full well that people sometimes insist, using a strange argument. If you allow, they say, that the missions are not absolutely necessary for the salvation of unbelievers, then you are taking away the best food for missionary zeal. But this argument is first of all too pragmatic. It is not a matter of arousing missionary zeal by any means whatsoever. That has to be founded on truth. The missionary must make his own the motives of the Church. His activity has to be inspired by the spirit of the Church whose messenger he is. Now it seems to me that there are in the true doctrine of the Church enough motives to nourish a most impassioned dedication to his work. Moreover, missionary activity that did not find its source in the motives of the Church could end up using methods and procedures that would not lead to the end desired by the Church. It would not be difficult to show what errors in practice this idea, that without the missions no salvation is possible for the "infidels," could lead to.

In the face of the morally unanimous affirmation of theologians that God offers the concrete means of salvation to every individual, people sometimes fall back on the following position. Salvation being more difficult for the infidel, they say, the missions are at least necessary to make it easier for him. I do not contest the fact that there is a certain truth in observations of this type. I do not wish to deny the difficulties encountered by the infidels, nor the help brought by Christianity. But in the last analysis, it is important also to recall the maxim of Christ: "From him to whom much has been given, much also shall be required." Saint Isidore of Seville said: "*Sub vetere Testamento, minoris culpae erant peccata, quia in eo non ipsa veritas, sed umbra veritatis aderat.*" * Why should this thought not be applied to those who find themselves in the infidel state without its being their fault? It might be asked if these ideas of "easier" and "more difficult" have any meaning here, and if they do not sometimes presuppose, in the background, a too confused, perhaps inexact idea of grace and freedom.

What seems to me true to say is that for each individual the revelation of the whole truth becomes the occasion of a more serious choice, and that the lights of this revelation, along with the means of salvation that are the Sacraments, permit him to go higher, but by the same token give him the obligation of doing so. What is brought to him by the Church is therefore not a greater facility for keeping himself in a sufficient mediocrity; it is the urgency of doing so, along with the means for going further. It is therefore necessary to base the necessity of the missions on the Church as such, before all else, on her nature and her role in mankind. It is necessary to see, by Faith, the designs of Divine Providence pursuing, by the action of grace, at once in the Church and in the parts of the human race that are still outside of her, one same plan of love and of mercy,

* "Under the Old Testament, sins were of a lesser guilt, because therein was not the truth itself, but the shadow of truth" (translation not in French ed.).

the reunion into a single Body of the entire saved humanity.

II. *Practical Consequences*

If it is a matter of permitting the original grace which is at work in a human group to materialize so that the entire Church may enrich herself from it; it cannot be a case of simply multiplying individual conversions. It is necessary to place at the heart of this human group everything that will really allow this particular form of grace to blossom out in the unity of the Church. That amounts to saying that the Church has to be implanted there, has to be organized in such a way as to be able to live, so to speak, on this capital; in such a way that little by little religious thought, a form of piety, a manner of realizing Christianity in practical life, which would have traits all their own in the great Catholic unity, are developed.

Whence comes the extreme importance assumed by the business of establishing not only a native clergy but also a native Hierarchy. You know that Benedict XV, and especially Pius XI, insisted greatly on that. Do not think that they considered that only as a "political" measure, even one inspired by very high motives—for example, making it easier to be converted to a religion preached by one's compatriots, or preserving the existence of Christianities in countries where the stranger risks no longer being admitted. Not at all. The guiding idea here is that each people must be called, within the interior of the Catholic Church, to make, in the highest degree possible, an original contribution. Passing through the mission stage is necessary; it may have to last a long time (and it is not for us, who are far from the concrete realities, to pass judgment on these questions of practical application); but it must be considered as essentially transitory. It is a help brought from without, but which has to aim at making itself useless. Missionary efforts really culminate on the day when, in a land where Christ has been announced, the Church is able to live without drawing on a foreign source. For all that there will not be any separation or isolation; among all the parts of the Catholic Church there must always be both the unity brought about by the Center, and the unity which results from interchanges. But for that it is necessary that the Church be truly implanted—which does not mean nationalized—it is necessary that she be truly grafted onto the wild tree to make it bear new fruit.

Whenever there is question of bringing grace to fruition, it will be necessary first of all to observe as much as possible in what direction it is growing. It will therefore be necessary to undertake a religious study of the people one desires to bring to the truth and integrate into the Church. Each missionary enterprise is an original case, and though there are general directives dictated by the very nature of the Church's mission, there is no method applicable everywhere. One has to know those one is getting ready to evangelize, to know their past efforts, their history, their doctrines; to go even into the sources of their civilization, to penetrate their own proper spirit: "Sympathetic knowledge," it is sometimes called, to underline that no unfavorable prejudice must be brought in. The expression, to tell the truth, does not fit, at least not completely. For what ultimately has to be studied amidst all sorts of human elements, is not a human effort; it is the secret conduct of grace.

Now, wherever grace is present, respect is seemly. It

is certainly not a case of blindfolding oneself so as not to see error or evil; or to have illusions regarding weaknesses or depravity; or to overestimate human possibilities. No, it is not all a case of that, but rather of guessing at a divine intention. For that matter there is never a whole that is so bad that all, absolutely all of it has to be rejected in a bloc. Far from it. One would have a poor understanding of the transcendance of Christianity if he thought that it obliges one to find no religious value outside the Christian revelation and the Catholic Church. Such an *a priori* would give a wrong orientation to the missionary effort.

Another consequence. Religious activity and human activity are certainly two different things. But they exist together, they are the products of the same men, and are not without some communication with one another. Likewise respect for the religious promise of a people— promise which is guessed at through what is already authentically religious in it—must entail respect for its whole patrimony of culture. Criticisms and reforms which will become necessary will have to imply this fundamental respect. Reviewing a work by Fr. Charles, recently, someone declared that he does not understand this statement, that it is "irreligious to destroy or sack the honest elements of a human culture, because one diminishes in this way wealth from the future patrimony of the Church." However it seems incontestable to me. All of that, you see, is a consequence of the way in which we have set up the basis of the missionary duty.

Conclusion

If in truth the activity of the Church is essential to her very being, it must be shared by all her members, by every Christian. It is not the specialty of a few, in which all the others would have no interest. Refusing to be associated with it would be to wish to be not of the Church, and to not want to live by her life.

That obviously has to be properly understood. It is not a case of imposing the same specialized task on each one, of sending everybody "to the missions." But the division of labor presupposes unity of the spirit. The Church's activity takes very different forms among her members, but these different forms have a solidarity among them, that is to say that a poor method of accomplishing one's own task will have repercussions everywhere. Some are called to leave everything: homeland, family, friends, to work effectively in a far-off mission. That is one of the highest forms of the Christian apostolate. It demands a great detachment, first of all by reason of the conditions of material life, which often will be hard; then, and above all, because it is necessary to become detached from one's manners of thinking, of feeling, of reacting, so as to enter as much as possible, into those of the men among whom one will have to live—an inward detachment, always necessary and much harder than the other because it affects much more profound areas of being. It is the negative facet of this adaptation, this assimilation to others, an indispensable condition for helping them to make the transition to conversion.

Indeed, there is no question of assimilating men to us under the pretext that we are Christians, in order to convert them to Christ. We are Christians in our way and they have to be such in their way. It is always, I repeat, it is always for us to free the grace working in them, to help them recognize it and sacrifice to it the evil they still cling to, to deliver it from all its shackles, which will happen only in the Church. But to help them in that way, to guide them, it is necessary first of all to have become as like them as possible, except for sin—in the image of Christ who became in all things like to us, except for sin.

After the example of Christ, the missionary is therefore inspired in all his efforts by the love of the men to whom he is sent. In edifying biographies we sometimes read that a certain religious—excellent man for all that— asked to go to the missions because it was the most arduous job. Whatever respect one may have for this attitude, it can be said to be little enlightened. If a person goes to the missions, it is out of love for those whom he is preparing to evangelize; it is even, preferably, out of love for the particular form of grace that is leading them on, drawn by the promise of all that the whole Church will reap from them, when they enter in. Because of that, a person accepts the required renunciations; one does not let himself be stopped by the natural obstacles that have to be overcome to answer the call of God. One even rejoices at having to suffer, following Christ's lead. But one does not seek out the missions first of all as a means of renunciation. Attraction for the missions has to be a work of grace, and since grace uses "secondary causes," it may happen that it will be born as the consequence of the knowledge one has arrived at regarding that which a human group, not as yet Christian, reveals of religious wealth, possibilities and promise in itself. The taste for such knowledge, a concern for acquiring it, is therefore a normal condition (I say "normal" because grace can make up for everything and sometimes does so) for the most fruitful missionary vo-

cations, those which will give missionaries who understand completely the greatness of their task.

Here, we touch upon the missionary duty of those
who remain. I am not forgetting that their first duty is
prayer (monetary aid to the missions must be added to
it). But this prayer must be born of an authentic missionary spirit, a spirit modeled on that of the Church herself.
If such a spirit is animating them, these Christians will
cause a missionary atmosphere to exist around them. The
Catholic masses will be preoccupied with the evangelization of the entire world, and their preoccupation will be
an enlightened one. The missionaries who leave reflect
for the most part, at least in some proportion—and it is
inevitable—the manner of seeing and feeling things of
their environment. Some, doubtless, can raise themselves
above it; again, it will often be because they will have
met some certain individual who will have led them to a
better understanding of their role.

It is therefore essential that in Christian countries there
be, diffused in the masses, a concern for universal evangelization; without it, missionary vocations stand every
chance of being rare. But it is also necessary that there
be a certain understanding of God's plan for our world,
that one think of this grace which is already working
obscurely in all peoples and which it is necessary to
bring to completion, so that these numerous vocations
might be also generous and fully enlightened. Therefore
people will keep themselves from making so many scorn-
ful and simplistic judgments on civilizations far removed
from ours, and without unfortunate complacency, will
know how to be fair to non-Christian religions.

Everything stands together: the quality of missionary
work, its right use, its profound efficacity, depend in

large measure on the quality of the missionary spirit which animates Christians, priests or laity, who live in Christian lands. In particular, it is necessary at all cost to avoid linking Catholicism to our ways of thinking and living, even to what is most legitimate in them. No doubt it is necessary that we, within the Church, have our way of being, our own style, but we are not to impose it on others; and so as not to risk doing so without our knowledge, it is a good idea to practice distinguishing the two things in our own conduct. It would indeed be a serious thing to make men, whoever they are, believe that in order to enter the Church, and share in the common salvation, they would have to renounce what they have—I say not only the right, but often the duty of preserving, for the very good of the Church. That would be to preach them a Christianity become at once heavier and deformed. *A fortiori* must we keep ourselves from making Catholicism consonant with what is still unchristian, unconverted, among us.